DOG TEAM TO
DAWSON

A QUEST FOR THE COSMIC BANNOCK
AND OTHER YUKON STORIES

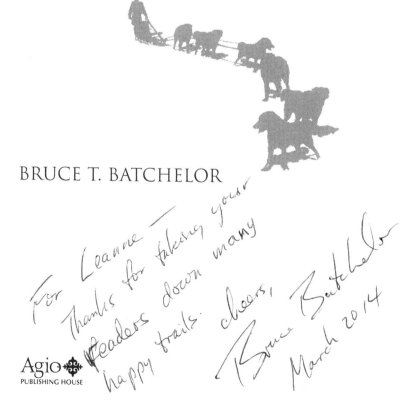

BRUCE T. BATCHELOR

Agio
PUBLISHING HOUSE

For Leanne —
Thanks for taking your
readers down many
happy trails. Cheers,
Bruce Batchelor
March 2014

DEDICATED to my best friend and soul-travelling buddy, Marsha

PUBLISHING HOUSE
151 Howe Street, Victoria BC Canada V8V 4K5

Cover and book design by Marsha Batchelor.
The photos accompanying *Trapping the Mad Trapper*
are from the Yukon Archives, Whitehorse, YK – Arthur
Thornthwaite and Claude & Mary Tidd collections.
All other photos are © Bruce Batchelor.
The author's mid-1970s winter travel was funded in part by
a Canada Council for the Arts Explorations Program grant.

Love Story for Lucy appeared in *The Lost Whole Moose
Catalogue* and in a later edition of *Yukon Channel Charts*.
Earlier versions of *Trapping the Mad Trapper* appeared in
Up Here and *Alaska* magazines.

For rights information and bulk orders, please go to
www.agiopublishing.com
Contact the author at *bruce.batchelor@gmail.com*

*Dog Team to Dawson: A Quest for the Cosmic Bannock
and other Yukon stories*
ISBN 978-1-927755-02-0 (trade paperback)
ISBN 978-1-927755-03-7 (ebook)
Cataloguing information available from
Library and Archives Canada.

Printed on acid-free paper.
Agio Publishing House is a socially responsible company,
measuring success on a triple-bottom-line basis.
10 9 8 7 6 5 4 3 2 1a

FOUR TRUE STORIES

DOG TEAM TO DAWSON:
A QUEST FOR THE COSMIC BANNOCK

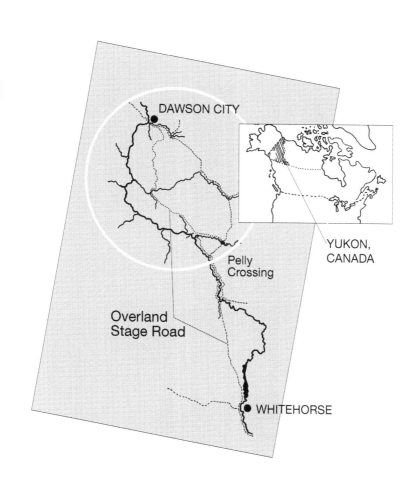

CHAPTER 1

DRIVING TO PELLY CROSSING

Doubts were intruding – no matter how I tried to ignore them – into my merry image of this adventure. The voices were those of close friends, parents. Even my own voice was there asking questions to which there were no easy answers: *This woman has never skied. She knows nothing about working with a dog team. How much help will she be on a 200-mile expedition? Are you crazy, man?*

Janet Prenty was concentrating on keeping her Datsun pickup truck from skating off the highway. Wet snow was steadily accumulating on the gravel road surface, hiding icy patches and disguising pot holes. Where the snow was level, it was about ankle-deep. In the wakes of the mammoth ore-hauling trucks with which we were sharing this road, packed snow had been moulded into humps higher than our pickup's differential and ruts far wider than our narrow wheelbase. Jan squinted at the world of white in front of us, straining to read the subtle differences in tone or hue that said 'packed snow here' or 'hiding under this dusting is a patch of black ice.'

In the headlights' brilliance, soggy flakes careened at us in a hypnotizing, 50-mile-a-hour kaleidoscope of patterns. There wasn't much I could do to help, so I leaned my head back, closed my eyes and tried not to let my doubts annoy and unnerve me. Jan was managing fine so far. She was certainly a crackerjack driver.

Yet she looked far too city-ish for this: pink skin, soft body, with golden blonde hair that won't survive two days away from a blow dryer. Guess I'd soon see how she coped with winter camping.

And what about yourself? You live in the Yukon for a few years and now think you can merrily recreate a long-abandoned trek to Dawson City with a pack of borrowed sled dogs and a Whitehorse barmaid? These dogs have never worked together as a team. What if they refuse to work? What if they tear each other to pieces and leave you stranded miles from nowhere?

Sure. True enough, I didn't have a lifetime of experience in the North. I'd grown up in ordinary southern Canadian cities, where I'd never even seen a dog team, never experienced 60-below-zero temperatures, and never travelled through the wilderness. Three years ago, right after graduating from university, I'd come to the Yukon Territory – fleeing from the very real prospect of being seduced into some computer job at a government bureaucracy or large corporation complicit in the Vietnam War. I came essentially for the promise of quick money to underwrite an escape overseas, but soon found that I loved the place! Short-term jobs, mostly in construction, surveying and mining, were dead easy to come by. The territory was populated with wild and wonderful characters, many of them perched on a bar stool ready to buy you a drink and fill your head with bush-life advice, tales of adventure, and confidences about sure-bet gold mines. During summer at the Arctic Circle, in this land of the midnight sun, that silly bright star tours clockwise all around the horizon, never rising very high in the sky but *never ever setting*. With all that constant daylight, many Yukoners simply worked and partied for months on end, seemingly postponing sleep until the long, dark winters.

I was fitting in perfectly. Those never-ending summer days were heaven to a never-grow-up, longhaired, 1970s hippie. I soon discovered that I could float a canoe down wide, briskly flowing rivers, paddling for weeks through landscapes of unimaginable beauty. Towering glacier-capped mountains, lush evergreen forests, moose- and mosquito-filled muskegs, emerald lakes… nothing in my public school geography lessons had even hinted at the magnificence of the Yukon Territory. I'd come fully prepared to find a flat tundra with scrawny black spruce and unmapped swamps. Instead, here were the highest mountains in Canada, a continuation of the Rocky Mountains. Here were tall and straight white spruce and lodgepole pine just begging to become walls of a log cabin – build one wherever you want. Here flowed the Yukon, one of the world's mightiest rivers, and dozens of intriguing tributaries. Two hundred thousand square miles with hardly any people, a land teeming with grizzly and black bear, beaver, moose, caribou, wolves and so many other critters. Overhead: whiskey jacks, owl, raven and eagles… How could anyone help but love the Yukon in summer?

Yes, but this is WINTER and you're about to set out on a trip with sled dogs you've never seen before and a woman you've barely met. Hardly a sane idea. Aren't you worried?

Truth be told, my experience using Northern husky dogs in harness was embarrassingly minimal. When those oh-so-ideal summer days had lapsed into the shorter, crisp days of autumn, I could still canoe until the dog salmon were running and the ice began to form. Then, although winter descended like an icy, dark blanket over the North, I found myself still thirsting at the well of adventure – determined to find a means of being mobile again out in that magical wilderness. Hiring a dog team and driver for a week was my first introduction to the mad world of Malamutes, Siberians and Samoyeds. I soon determined dogs were noisy, often uncooperative, and consumed enormous quantities of food whether they were being used or not. They were prone to fighting at the slightest provocation, and required a year-round commitment by their owner. At least five dogs, preferably more, were needed to pull a complete outfit, especially when travelling anywhere off the beaten path. And unless the trail was packed and near perfect, one person had to half-run, half-steer the toboggan while another person had to walk, snowshoe or ski, breaking trail ahead of the dogs.

Cross-country skiing with a backpack was a much better match with my temperament. If I could have one dog following me, dragging a lightly-loaded toboggan, there would be relative quiet, no dog fights, less dog food consumed, no hired dog driver and only a pet to mind in the off-season. Who'd want to look after a yard full of huskies all spring, summer and fall? Right when you could be off canoeing? Imagine the cost just to feed them!

For two winters, I'd been content to scout around on skis, taking short jaunts into the bush with one dog. Sometimes I'd visit a trapper at his cabin, someone I'd met on his occasional supply run into town, or young homesteaders who'd created their own personal Walden in the wilderness. On each trip I picked up tips on how to be comfortable with simple light equipment. Soon I was packing two sleeping bags but no tent. Yet no matter how I pared down my camping outfit, winter food rations for man and beast weighed a lot, meaning that about six days was the limit to how far this man-on-skis-and-one-dog-with-small-sled arrangement could go.

Call it a basic character flaw maybe, where reason can become a casualty to impulse, but I have never been too keen on *limits*. Despite my logical determination to not own a dog team, I'd recently been getting strange nudges and visual flashes about the winter route taken three-quarters of a century before by dog teams delivering the mail from the coast to the Klondike. Imagine mushing a dog team to Dawson! I could try the northern leg of this route, starting from Pelly Crossing and travel the frozen rivers to Dawson City – that was a particularly picturesque journey I'd canoed in summer. Clearly my lightweight one-dog touring style wouldn't be enough. The distance of over 200 miles with lots of unpacked trail meant a full dog team – or even two – would be necessary.

Yet I had no dog team, no money for supplies, not even a sled. And no partner to share the rugged work of trail breaking and winter camping. I'd reluctantly resigned myself to passing up or postponing this idea, perhaps even taking up a surveying job for a few months, when an encouraging string of coincidences occurred.

One night last week, in Whitehorse's raunchy Edgewater Tavern, obstacles to this journey evaporated one by one into the smoky air. First was the lack of a partner.

Jan Prenty, a pretty and spunky waitress, studied me for a long time before tentatively sitting on the edge of an empty chair across from me. Her intense stare made me wonder if I had beer foam on my moustache or potato chip crumbs in my beard. Both were quite likely.

She then glanced around, checking the other tables in her duty area, and said simply, "I want you to take me winter camping."

My drinking companion gagged on his beer. Three-Quarter Jon

Rudolph's eyes watered slightly as he struggled for control. Only through great effort did he prevent himself from extruding his present foamy mouthful through his nose.

"You've got to be kidding," was all I could think of to say. She'd caught me completely off guard. Though I'd met Jan before, we'd never said much more than hello. This sudden request had an embarrassing touch of double entendre to it; colour was rising in my cheeks.

"Why should I be kidding? I've camped in the summer," she said. "You're always going off on trips to someone's trapline. I'd like to see what it's like to camp in the winter, that's all."

She was clearly intent on going camping. I mumbled something about travelling over the old dog team mail route to Dawson City. It was a journey oft-discussed in the bars, but it hadn't been attempted with dogs in many decades.

"Unfortunately, though, it would require a team of at least six dogs," I said. "And money for dog food and supplies. And transportation to take everything to Pelly Crossing. And dog harnesses. And a toboggan. And it would be very hard work. And it is getting too late in the season."

Having finally regained his composure, Jon interrupted to offer two dogs and a makeshift toboggan. He then gave me a lewd wink to indicate he'd be quite happy to take Jan into the bush instead.

"And I have a truck," Jan pointed out.

"Half a truck," corrected Jon, never one to hide his biases. "That little rice-burner can't haul half the load of a real pickup—"

At that moment, an envelope with three $20 bills arrived at our table, having been passed hand-to-hand across the room from somewhere in the corner. "That's the fifty you lent me last August, Bruce," Jim called out. "Plus a bit of interest!" A group of young, long-haired miners from Keno Hill laughed approvingly at their red-headed buddy's comment.

"There you go. Cash for the dog food," Jan said merrily. "And I've got a credit card for gas. I don't know how to ski. So you'll have to teach me. Now we just need more dogs, right?"

Jeez, it is downright freaky when pieces of a puzzle fall into place so quickly. John Tapsell from Dawson City leaned over from the adjoining table and offered to lend his three dogs. He had three big brutes who could use some exercise. They hadn't ever been really trained, he cautioned, but surely the right person could get some use out of them.

Not to be outdone, Mike Cowper piped up to volunteer his pet husky, Tuk, for whatever trip it was we were discussing. Suddenly I had seven dogs including my own Casey, plus an over-eager rookie female partner… and no more obstacles, except hundreds of miles of abandoned trail, river ice and all the blizzards and demons that the Yukon could throw at us. I felt a bit trapped. And too embarrassed to back out.

"Go for it, Bruce! To Dawson City!" Jon raised his glass, then told Jan to bring another round.

Coincidences. Your life seems to run on luck, said those voices. *What if this romp ends in some epic Jack London-ish disaster? Get her to turn this pickup around right now.*

"Someone has to be confident," I muttered.

Jan turned her head partially in my direction while keeping her eyes locked on the road ahead. "Did you say something?" she asked.

Her next words were drowned out by the horrifically loud rasping of packed snow scraping on the underside of the pickup truck. We'd run into another snow-drifted section and Jan had to wrestle to keep the Datsun's nose pointed north. The light truck planed over the dense drift, sledding on its oil pan, wheels spinning frantically. Jan twitched the steering wheel to correct for a slight sideways skid, but kept her foot hard on the gas pedal. I noticed her knuckles were white. Seconds later, the drifted portion abruptly ended and all was normal again – if driving on a snow- and ice-covered gravel highway through a blizzard can be called normal.

She'll probably give up after one day out.

"I said, 'Do you think we can make it to Dawson with these dogs?' "

"Why not?" she asked back. "You getting worried? I can keep up, you know."

"Naw, it'll be great. Like a *holiday*."

That last word rang in my ears as I stared ahead into the mesmerizing snow swirls. My voice was surprisingly confident; my gut was in a painfully fierce knot.

CHAPTER 2

SEVEN SLEEPERS

Ssshhh! Sh!

Imagine yourself peeking in on seven mixed-breed sled dogs sleeping peacefully under the canopy shell on Jan's pickup truck's box. Lulled into tranquillity by the vibrations and constant droning of tires churning over the snow and gravel, they appear quite harmless, even pet-cute. Through the cab's rear window, we can examine them one-by-one. They are the strange result of breeding near-savage Northern work dogs with various southern domestic breeds. It's a stew pot of instincts, temperaments and body structures. Each serving is very different...

There are faint wisps of frosty breath rising from each wet nose. Six are black, while the seventh nose is pink, like a pencil eraser. Curled into an orange and white fur ball against the cab is my own pet, Casey the Wonder Dog. He is almost two and weighs about sixty-five pounds. This wild-eyed, eraser-nosed, Malamute-collie cross will serve as our lead dog. He understands commands for 'gee' [turn right] and 'haw' [turn left] from pulling a sled during previous camping outings.

Snuggled against Casey is another Malamute cross: Iskoot, who is about the same age and stature, but all white. One of Iskoot's paws is twitching – likely chasing Arctic hares in his dreams.

"Iskoot's not very confident yet about leading," Jon had reported. "He's too shy. Hope he grows out of it – maybe this trip will help."

Jon's other loaner was our sole female, the regal Mitti. She's arranged herself so her chin is resting on my blue pack; her long, silky, white coat and smooth head give her the look of an over-sized spaniel. Like Iskoot, she has a few days of experience in harness, and is purportedly "a good worker, unless she spots a damn squirrel – then she barks her f**king head off."

Tuk is sprawled on top of the brown tarpaulin, no doubt laying claim to the dog food beneath – 40 pounds of beef fat and 125 pounds of kibble pellets – enough for 10 to 14 days. Tuk has a wolf's head, massive chest, narrow hips and high, curled tail – he could appear on postcards as a 'mighty Northern Husky.' He fits that stereotype. According to his owner Mike, he is a rather spoiled pet who has Samoyed and Malamute blood lines. I'd borrowed Tuk once earlier in the winter. He was strong but quite sucky, needing lots of reassurance. Tuk is sleeping fitfully with one ear cocked towards the three newcomers who might dispute his position above the food.

At the back, John Tapsell's three dogs are jammed into a familial fur pile on the toboggan. It is hard to tell where one dog ends and another begins, except that the shaggy white hair must belong to Sherlock, the thick black coat to his littermate, Rafferty, and the shorter, tan and black patches are Flander. All three are novices to this mushing business.

Sherlock has become a well-known dog this winter, a minor celebrity, for his strange talent of eating dog houses. He could calmly munch through plywood, particle board or lumber, tearing out nails and staples with his teeth, reducing a dog house to a few wood and iron scraps and a large pile of dog doo. John was studying for his carpenter's papers and apparently welcomed the opportunity to design each successive mini-house project, practising diminutive gable windows on one, hipped roofs on the next, and gingerbread trim on another. While we were away, John would study the theoretical aspects of his chosen trade.

Brother Rafferty's sole previous outing in harness was a spur-of-the-moment entry in a one-dog weight-pulling contest at the Mayo winter carnival. John hadn't been able to interest Rafferty in pulling at all until a little girl wandered out of the crowd ahead of his dog. Rafferty barked, wagged his tail and, seemingly without effort, dragged the six-hundred-pound sled towards the child. John quickly escorted the child across the finish line with Rafferty hard on their heels, tail still a-wagging.

Harnessed to a slightly heavier load a few moments later, Rafferty showed a distinct lack of interest in either the contest or the girl. Apparently the black dog had received all the hugs and pats he wanted from the tiny human and was quite content to sit beside the sled and grin at the cheering and jeering spectators. John's advice, based on his dog's brief pulling career: "Rafferty'll work hard if you can motivate him. You just have to find out how."

The third of this trio is smaller, but the obvious ring-leader. Perhaps it is his German shepherd heritage that makes Flander look so sly, even when sleeping. That, and his hang-down ears and long, wiener-like tail.

Now, imagine them all. There are six curled, bushy, husky-dog tails and a single thin, black, straight one. All these tails are still. Each dog is dozing to the monotone drone of a small truck driving to Pelly Crossing. Each canine brain is monitoring the sounds, the smells, and vibrations

– likely even the other dogs' thoughts – while the muscular body rests, preserving energy, keeping warm.

Think of them as cute if you like, but this peace won't last much longer. Let's let them sleep while the Datsun emerges from the blizzard and rumbles on through the afternoon.

Sh-sh-sh.

CHAPTER 3

TRAILHEAD

Just after 4 p.m., we crossed the Pelly Crossing bridge. The moment Jan down-shifted and steered onto the left shoulder, we could feel our cargo coming alive. Seven bodies herded from window to window in anticipation of an early parole. Mitti's frantic, high-pitched, staccato barking would surely be pumping the team's adrenalin.

My door was open before the wheels were completely stopped, and I bounded out to unlock the canopy hatch. Keeping seven loose sled dogs in such a small space was asking for trouble.

"Any blood?" Jan called back just as a 500-pound fur ball knocked me over like a bowling pin and left me spinning on the snow. The mass immediately split into seven boneheads attached to individual bodies, each exploding into a full gallop. Paws thundered down the trail, tails flagged a good-bye, and in seconds… we were alone.

I examined the surrounding snow for any red spots.

"No signs of trouble," I reported, then scanned the truck interior. "No blood in here either!"

Dog team owners typically use multiple-unit, portable 'dog boxes' when transporting their dogs, even when all the dogs know one another. A truck-box-sized plywood kennel is divided into small compartments each just big enough for one dog and each cell has its own latched door. Ten-dog kennels, and even the occasional double-decker, 20-dog unit, are familiar sights on Yukon roads. We'd taken quite a gamble hauling our team without one, really pushing our luck, but had apparently won this toss.

"This is it?" Jan asked, pointing to the single-lane road down which our dogs had disappeared. "The road to Pelly Farm?"

"This is it. Next stop Dawson City. Estimated time of arrival: eight to ten days from now. Twelve days max."

From here at the highway crossing over the Pelly River, we would follow an unploughed, 32-mile, one-lane road to an isolated farm near the Pelly's confluence with the Yukon River. Past that point we would use the river itself for our trail.

"Those dogs better come back to pull us," Jan laughed.

"Yeah!" I agreed. "I'll feel much better as soon as we're ten minutes down the trail and really on our way."

The new snow was about four inches deep over the last tracks on the side road, and very sticky. The afternoon high had been well above freezing, but as the sun was sinking lower in the south-west, one could feel the temperature dropping. The sky was now clear and it would be cold soon.

We began to unload our outfit, beginning with the toboggan. I put some sticks on the ground beside the truck and we lifted the toboggan out and onto them. This would keep the toboggan from freezing fast while we loaded up. Next, we stretched out the harnesses in the order I figured would work best. Casey's first, then Iskoot's because he needed to learn about leading, then—

Parked near the Pelly River bridge, we are packing hundreds of pounds of gear and supplies on the toboggan.

Suddenly all hell broke loose. Dog fight! Growling and squealing, six dogs had locked into a rolling, snapping brawl. Teeth were flashing and tufts of fur floated up into the air. The din was terrifying. My heart pounded as I fought the immediate impulse to insert myself between the combatants. Sherlock and Rafferty twisted and grappled, their faces splattered with blood. Above them, Casey and Flander wrestled, jaws clenched vise-like on each other's fur. Tuk and Iskoot were indiscriminately biting any limb that came their way. Only Mitti stood apart from the pile, barking frantically. Jan began shrieking, "STOP IT! STOP IT!" as loud as she could, but no one was listening.

I grabbed Iskoot's collar and hurled him aside. Across the fray, Jan seized Tuk by the back of his neck and yanked him free. The next pair scattered as soon as they realized the humans were involved, but our two most serious scrappers had to be literally pried apart with a stick. When finally Jan held Sherlock and I his brother, they glared at each other for a moment, then started to wag their tails!

I looked up at Jan. She grimaced and shook her head.

"That was scary," she said simply. "I hope it never happens again."

"Scares the hell out of me too when dogs do that," I admitted. My hands were shaking noticeably. "Let's hope they've got their pecking order sorted out now."

Rafferty had red all over his face, but there was no obvious source until Jan pointed out the stained snow around Sherlock's feet. A deep gash across one pad was gushing blood each time he took a step. Jan bundled him off to the truck to see what she could do, leaving me with the other six.

"Holidays are over," I declared, putting harnesses on and adding each dog to the single file forming ahead of the toboggan. As soon as they were hooked up, John Tapsell's remaining two rookies immediately began gnawing at the leather straps and testing the limits of their confinement. I was in no mood to repair chewed harnesses and slapped their ears with my leather gauntlet mitt to tell them so. Big brawling Rafferty instantly transformed into a whimpering mess, peeing on himself, terrified by my every move, and desperately anxious to climb back into the truck.

Tuk was growling at Rafferty, Mitti re-started her maddening barking, Casey had turned around and was playing with Iskoot, their traces now a mass of tangles, and Flander was licking my boot.

I took a big sigh. How are we ever going to get this ridiculous excuse-for-a-team to Dawson? I wondered, shaking my head.

According to Jan, Sherlock's bleeding had stopped, but would re-start as soon as he put any weight on it. We were faced with our first crisis and hadn't even finished unloading the truck!

I'd no experience with a dog cutting his pad before and really no way of gauging the degree of seriousness of Sherlock's injury. Dogs have remarkable mending processes, but this wound was in a critical place. He certainly wouldn't be able to pull worth a damn until it healed. Jan and I stared at each other, hoping for inspiration, when the sound of an approaching pickup turned on light bulbs in our heads.

Only after we'd flagged it to an icy stop did we recognize the driver: Dan Buckles, neighbour of Sherlock's owner.

"We're in a bit of a jam, Dan. Can you help out?" I asked. "One of our dogs is cut up and has to be returned to John Tapsell. What do you think about Sherlock hitching a ride with you?"

Moments later, from his perch atop a load of lumber, Sherlock disappeared down the highway, wagging his tail and sniffing the rushing air.

We didn't waste time lamenting his departure. Jan and I got back to work, shuffling our outfit from truck to toboggan and lashing it all in place. Somehow we found room on our small toboggan for all the dog food, about eighty pounds of our food and kitchen gear, 20-ish pounds of bedding, maybe 30 pounds of clothes and perhaps 30 more pounds of tools, tarpaulin, light dog chains and other odds and ends. Including a musher, the team would be pulling over 450 pounds, with the only consolation being that the load would steadily lighten with each meal served.

Jan drove off to park her truck at the Pelly Crossing village gas station, leaving me alone with the six remaining dogs who were now peacefully sprawled out in the snow, yawning and licking at their minor tears and bruises. The plan was for me to work the team for the first few miles and Jan would follow on foot in a few minutes. I untangled the harnesses for what seemed like the fiftieth time, gave a mighty heave and told Casey, "Let's GO!"

The toboggan lurched forward, pushing up loose snow and crunching and grinding over lumps of ice. Rafferty and Flander in particular leaned enthusiastically into their traces as we swept away along the road. It was now six-thirty and sunset would be around eight. A huge advantage to travelling in April would be the ever-lengthening days. We'd start with over 14 hours between sunrise and sunset and add five minutes more every day. With so much snow cover to reflect light, dawn and dusk would be fairly bright also.

The farm access road is on the north side of this east-west Pelly River valley, winding at first through an area devastated by a fire a decade ago. It was a black and white, high-contrast scene of burnt trees, with stubbled branches and strips of blackened bark clinging to the grey trunks, all trimmed in fluffy white flakes. Snow-drifted caps on stump tops were like oversized mushrooms in this bleak forest. Gray stalks of dried fireweed protruded lifeless from ice patches. All was ghostly quiet save for the rustling of traces and the raspy, snow-crunching prow of the toboggan.

A large truck's double tires had packed deep ruts on this road, each track just narrower than the toboggan. Even though I stopped the dogs repeatedly and placed them bodily one by one on the centre mound between the ruts, they refused to run there and immediately the toboggan was dragged again into a rut, one edge in and the other riding the rim so the load was in constant danger of tipping. When it did topple, only by crouching low and heaving as hard as I could with my shoulder was I able to right the load. Mushing along this rutted section was curiously like tacking a small sailboat: I hung onto one handlebar and hiked way to the side to keep our craft from listing over too far.

The road initially followed the lip of a cliff above the Pelly, then turned up a creek gulch that had escaped the fire. Occasionally there was a spectacular view of the river but just as often the road was walled in by pine and spruce forest. At the first uphill, I stepped off as the toboggan slowed and walked behind. Gradually progress diminished to the point where I began pushing on the handlebars and shouting encouragement. Nearing the top, as we were losing all momentum, I put my shoulder against the load and leaned with all my strength. With each step I dug my boots into the snow for traction and strained to help.

"Come on, Casey!" I encouraged. "Let's go! We can make it! Mush! Mush!"

Just before the crest of the hill, I glanced up and saw that the traces behind Tuk, the wheel dog, were slack and all the dogs' tails were up and wagging merrily! They had all caught on to this game very quickly, it seemed – far quicker than I had. They were happily looking back, watching me do all the work.

When I too let up, we stopped immediately. I walked up to Tuk and shouted "WORK!" in his ear as loudly as I could. He jumped sideways as far as his traces allowed and cowered. I repeated this performance with each dog and what it lacked in surprise was more than offset by the dreaded anticipation.

Now, when I returned to the toboggan and called out, "Let's GO," all six bodies leaned heartily into their harnesses and we were once more underway, crunching onwards. I was able to ride again, scanning the passing terrain for a suitable camping spot.

Soon I found a sheltered, flat patch under a massive spruce, just room enough for two sleeping bags and our packs on the mossy ground. Within easy reach were a half-dozen three-inch-diameter spars for firewood, and six stout trees to which the dogs would be chained. There was no creek, but we could melt snow for our drinking water. I whoaed the dogs and was digging out their chains when Jan danced into camp wearing her moccasins with toe rubbers over them, carrying both parkas and an armful of other items we'd left behind in the cab of her Datsun.

She had colour in her cheeks and a big hello for each dog. There ensued a tremendous clamour as each dog tried to tell her about being deaf in one ear. Jan didn't understand a thing they told her but won their hearts by patting heads and rubbing chins.

I chopped up firewood while Jan dug out supper food from the big kitchen box. Soon we had steaks, eggs and onions frying, the tea billy boiling, and were able to pause for a moment before feeding the dogs their crunchies.

With the sunset now fading, a rising full moon cast a silver-blue iridescent glow over our snow-carpeted campsite. I caught Jan's eye for a moment and we exchange smiles. During all the unpacking and setting up, we'd worked steadily and effectively, conversing in short, necessary sentences. I realized suddenly that neither of us had taken the time to really notice the other person or to inquire about the other's feelings.

"I'm glad you wanted to come along," I offered over the crackling fire.

"Well," she laughed, "I'm glad, too!" And then she looked at me through the steam rising from her mug and added, "Partner."

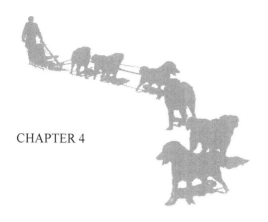

CHAPTER 4

RAFFERTY'S STRANGE LOVE

There was 20 degrees of frost in the clear morning air when I wiggled out of my sleeping bag and fumbled into my clothes. Taking advantage of the generous supply of squaw wood – the lower, dead branches – on the tree we'd slept under, I soon had a hot fire snapping, its smoke drifting through the dense forest.

As I warmed my fingers, one by one the dogs lifted their heads from the snow nests they'd dug, stretched their necks and said hello. Each made a tentative woof, like a singer tuning his vocal chords, until finally, with Casey as opening soloist, the morning greetings became a full-blown symphony of howls. Mitti, who didn't seem to be able to howl, offered her choppy, high-pitched bark, playing an effective counterpoint to the con brio improvisations of the five wannabe wolves around her.

Though others may find huskies' howling eerie or even scary, something inside me was amused by their primeval yodelling and I couldn't stop smiling. Watching the over-earnest expressions on their doggy faces as each one contorted and strained and rolled his eyes back – their seriousness triggered tears of laughter rolling down my cheeks. I found myself cheering, "Louder! More noise! More!" as I savoured the silly racket.

The sleeping bag shuddered twice, erupted a mop of matted blonde hair, then began squirming like a puffy, ringed caterpillar. Moments later a half-dressed Jan half-emerged and sat up rubbing sleep from her eyes.

"Does this mean it's morning?" she asked in a groggy voice when the dogs paused. "It's sure hard to sleep in with all that racket."

"Seven-thirty and all's well," I laughed. "Let's get at 'er while the snow's still crisp."

The toboggan would slide much more easily over the icy crust now coating yesterday's snowfall. If the temperature later in the day rose above freezing again, we would be in for some sticky trail conditions.

Stopping only to warm our fingers, eat some rye bread and sip last night's coffee from the thermos, we brushed the frost off our bedding and rolled and packed and tied and were soon priming and harnessing the workers. Now steeped, the hot tea went into the thermos to drink later. Strangely, neither Rafferty nor Mitti had eaten all their food from last night so Tuk opportunely vacuumed up the unwanted crunchies as he was escorted past their nest spots to his place in the traces. That would be the last time that any of the dogs left any food uneaten.

As a pick-me-up – and a bribe – we distributed chunks of beef fat to the team. Each ration was swallowed almost without chewing. This fat would balance the high-protein racing formula dry food we'd brought for their evening meals.

Tuk was showing the most energy, so I moved him up to lead position and we lurched off down the trail. Our camping spot had been only three miles in from the highway and I was eager to cover a decent distance today, taking us at least half the way to Pelly Farm.

Jan buckled her brand new boots into the cross-country skis and, holding the gee-line [a trailing rope], was towed behind like a water skier. Instead of coping with a motorboat's wake, though, she had to navigate the tire ruts. After only a few spills, she got the hang of it and became quite adept.

On the uphills I stepped off and walked behind, lending a hand on the steepest parts and encouraging the dogs to "Get UP! Let's GO!" On the downhills I stood on the brake so as not to run down Mitti, today's wheel dog. Our brake was a metal claw bolted to a plywood pad, in turn hinged to the tail of the toboggan. My weight on the pad caused the claw to furrow deeply into the snowy trail, ploughing yet another rut Jan had to contend with.

Rafferty's leg near his ankle was stiff and tender around a gash from yesterday's fight and he let out a yelp whenever he put too much strain on it. I encouraged him to lick the wound clean but he didn't comprehend the fuss at all. Only Flander understood my concern and he licked it for his buddy whenever we paused to untangle twisted harnesses.

After an hour of steady progress, during a steep descent with the dogs galloping strongly, the plywood brake pad snapped in two. By tipping the toboggan on its side, I managed to stop it and save Mitti from being overtaken and crushed. I'd forgotten, however, that I was not the last in this procession. A split second later, Jan slammed into me from behind, wrapping arms, legs, poles and skis around me as we somersaulted over the backboard into the toboggan's basket.

"Oops," she said sheepishly as the stars settled.

"Oops," I agreed, laughing.

Ahead of us, six dogs wagged their tails in agreement and smiled their goofy, tongue-hanging-out dog-grins.

"I think I've a few things yet to learn about making toboggan brakes," I admitted.

"I think we've got a lot to learn about *everything*," Jan said matter-of-factly.

She poured tea from the thermos while I wired the brake claw directly to the hinge as a makeshift brake. The temperature had risen noticeably over the past hour – I was using the pliers without mitts.

"With the sun warming this south-facing side of the valley and melting our crust, we may not need a brake much this afternoon," I suggested. "Our trouble will be sliding on sticky snow, not stopping."

Taking advantage of the pause, Flander was snoring softly, his head leaning against Rafferty's butt, who was making low disagreeable noises at Tuk at the opposite end of the line. Iskoot was wriggling around on his back, rubbing an itch while Casey had wrapped himself up like a mummy in his traces. Mitti posed very regally, surveying the rabble in front of her, then settled down to lick snowballs from between the brown pads of her feet.

Our team sported an eclectic collection of harnessing, provided by the dogs' owners; each was a bit different in style, age and state of repair. Gold rush era freighting harnesses – designed for use on narrow trails and hauling a load – were scaled-down tandem horse harnesses, with padded collars to which heavy leather straps called traces were attached. We had only one collar harness: Casey's. The other dogs' harnesses had a wide leather band across the front of the dog's chest, and another strap around the back and tummy to hold the traces in position. Each dog's traces were clipped to the following dog's harness, so they were in a single file about 60 feet long. I'd put spare belting, a leather punch, waxed heavy cotton thread and an awl in the tool kit to repair the inevitable breakage. Plus we had Sherlock's harness as a spare.

Determined to squeeze every mile possible from the crust, we moved on as soon as the brake repair was complete. By now we'd left behind the scattered burnt-off patches of forest and were paralleling the river through tall straight poplars. Here, the packed snow on the road averaged about six inches deep, so it would take many days yet to melt completely, especially in the shade. On the sidehill above us, though, all loose snow was gone. Green grass shoots hadn't appeared yet in those bare patches, but the sight of bare earth was unnerving – a blunt reminder that this trip was running on a very tight timetable. Spring was coming on fast; we had less than three weeks before the weather would become uncomfortably hot for these furry dogs to work, the trail too slushy (or muddy), and the river ice too dangerous for travelling. I was hoping we could dash through in ten days.

Two miles on, Mitti's harness suddenly snapped. The old leather fastenings weren't up to the strain of six dogs pulling ahead while the toboggan yanked back.

Jan sat on the toboggan curl to dig out the spare harness for Mitti. Rafferty, momentarily freed, immediately walked over to Jan, lifted his leg high and peed profusely on her shoulder.

I seized Rafferty, shaking him violently, yelling, "NO! NO! NO!"

I was afraid to look at Jan, worried how she'd react. Would she freak out? But when I did take a peek, she was grinning at me and holding back laughter!

"Something to tell your grandchildren about someday?" I teased, placing a handful of snow on her coat to absorb the urine.

"Yeah, but maybe I'll leave out some of the details," she muttered while brushing off the yellow snow.

Rafferty sat gazing vacantly at Jan, wagging his great curled tail slowly back and forth. He didn't appear at all repentant. In fact, he gave the impression of a complete absence of thought, a total void behind those dark, cow-eyes. Quite possibly he was in love with Ms. Prenty.

We'd just started again when we reached a flooded section of the road. About an inch of new ice had formed over six inches of water where a spring was creating a minor glacier across our route.

There was no way around; the road was flanked tightly in dense willows. So we paused to catch our breath, rolled our eyes at each other, nodded, then rushed forward, cheering on the dogs.

Toenails clattered, digging into the ice as we raced for the far side. But ten feet short of success, the toboggan caught on a ridge, spinning sideways. Then it toppled over, breaking the surface and sinking into the icy water.

Jan and I heaved it back upright as quickly as possible and dragged it forward to the first dry patch. There we assessed the water penetration, hauling bundles and bags out of the tarpaulin-wrapped cargo area. Our food was fine except for one somewhat soggy rye bread loaf. The paper dog food bags, however, were wet and one side of the bedding roll was damp.

Jan's ski boots were soaked from rescuing the toboggan but she said that didn't matter. "Let's just carry on," she said gamely. "I'm actually curious to find out what will go wrong next!"

About a third of the way to Pelly Farm, before Braden's Canyon, the road bends away from the Pelly River and climbs up along a ravine. The dogs didn't appreciate the incline and seized every possible excuse to stop. Each dog took a separate turn to have a bowel movement, causing more back-breaking work for me to re-start the toboggan in this sticky snow and steer around the steaming deposit.

Frustration was building for all of us when another broken harness trace forced a halt. This time there was no intact spare and my repair would take twenty minutes. While I cobbled, Jan fixed rye and cheese sandwiches, the dogs watching her attentively.

Our spirits picked up after a snack and, with clearer minds, we decided to look for a good spot to rest for the afternoon. Ideally, it would be somewhere bare of snow under a big white spruce, in the sun, where we could dry out from the morning dunking and wait for the temperature to drop again.

With that setting clearly in our minds, we got the dogs up from their nap and pushed off again up the steep hill. Both of us were straining to help move the load: coaxing, shouting, pulling, bullying, then stopping. Then back to grunting, leaning, heaving, sweating. I was stripped down to a T-shirt under the blazing sun, my skin tingling from the radiation reflecting off the snow. After one gruelling mile, the dogs would have no more of it and we were exhausted.

Thus we were halted once more, for what would likely be at least four hours, in the middle of this slushy road, on an uphill slope with nothing but scruffy black spruce for neighbours. There was no bare ground in sight, no creek for running water – certainly this was not the site I'd envisioned.

I spread the tarpaulin to lie upon and stretched wet and damp clothes around us to dry in the sun. Jan pulled pans from the kitchen box and put a thin layer of snow in each. Twenty minutes later the sun had done its business and we had a few mouthfuls of stale-tasting water to sip. Jan sprinkled orange juice powder over more snow, creating a mush that was unsettlingly reminiscent of Rafferty's earlier performance. The melt time was much shorter, but to make this coloured melt-water palatable we needed a wee dram of Scotch whisky from our repair kit.

Like Hansel and Gretel's trail of bread crumbs, dog food had been trickling out from a small tear, so Jan rough-stitched a sturdier sack from a length of canvas, and then transferred the crunchies. At the first rattle, six pairs of eyes were locked on her every move.

The toboggan needed repairs, too. The frequent tipping had loosened the plywood sidewalls but that was nothing that some haywire and twists of the pliers couldn't rectify. Noticing a few loose bolts, I shook my head and wondered if this clumsy affair would really make it to Dawson. How did I get talked – or talk myself – into believing Jon's jury-rigged toboggan would work for the ten or more days ahead of us?

The toboggan's base was a child's toy made of thin slats of hardwood, seven feet long and designed to carry perhaps three pre-schoolers down an icy suburban Ontario slope. Before an earlier trip, Three-Quarter Jon and I had replaced the original thin crossbars with strips of 3/4-inch plywood. Jon then welded four steel braces so I could bolt on spruce pole handlebars. The handlebars were wired to the front curl and we loosely wove a net of rope along each side to contain the load. Inside this net, to protect the contents from poking branches or rasping ice chunks, were thin plywood panels. On the toboggan's base I'd painted three coats of urethane and a thick layer of paraffin wax – much of which, I was sure, was already sanded off by the abrasive snow crust.

"Wouldn't a sleigh with runners be better than a toboggan?" Jan asked, interrupting her stitching to cut us chunks from a garlic sausage ring. "There would be much less bottom to drag on this sticky snow."

"Much better, yes," I agreed. "But when we hit deep or unpacked snow later on, a sleigh would sink and catch where a flat-bottomed toboggan will stay on top. My main worry is that we're going to wear right through the base on the icy sections."

"Then what will we do?" she asked.

"I hope we'll be close enough to Dawson by that time to be back on a packed trail. Somehow we'll attach the skis under the toboggan as runners. I brought eight long bolts just in case."

"Sounds good to me," Jan smiled, buttoning up her parka and leaning back to catch a faceful of sunshine. "With no skis, I'll have to ride!"

The sudden cold woke us a few hours later. As the sun moved along the horizon and cast the narrow, tree-lined ravine into shade, the temperature had instantly dropped 15 degrees. We quickly gathered the clothes and tarp, and straightened out the inevitable harness tangle. I led on skis with Jan nervously taking her first tour of duty as musher. Iskoot was our latest candidate for lead dog and he threw himself into the job with enthusiasm, rallying the dogs to pull the toboggan smartly on the newly chilled road surface.

With Casey right behind him to interpret any gee or haw, the skinny white pup only had to understand 'get up' and 'whoa.' Jan, however, kept singing, "Let's Go-oo-oo-oo" at the dogs as they trotted along, causing great confusion because half of them thought this was the hoped-for "whoa-whoa-whoa." After I offered this explanation, Jan walked from dog to dog, having a lengthy heart-to-heart conversation with the bemused canines. Every dog wagged his tail and panted and appreciated the scratches that accompanied her lecture. And, despite my initial scepticism about this approach, Jan soon had them pulling well and apparently understanding exactly what she meant.

Out in front I could now relax and enjoy the skiing. We slid out of the ravine and onto a stretch of gentler slopes. After the raucous crust-rasping noise at the toboggan's tail, I savoured the comparative tranquillity of swishing skis and faint creaking of bamboo poles. It was exhilarating to be gliding effortlessly through the poplar forest, noticing snow grouse trying to be invisible and squirrels playing in the branches. Relishing the random glimpses of snow-crust-covered river far below flashing in the late-afternoon sun – all confirming why I so loved to be out travelling in the winter and early spring. I became so involved in the scenery and fun of skiing that twice when the toboggan tipped I was out of ear-shot, leaving Jan on her own to heave the heavy load upright. She managed fine until the third time when the upset was downhill, slightly off the road and tight against a willow thicket. After a valiant effort, she sat on the load fuming until I noticed their absence behind me. I skied a half-mile back rather sheepishly to lend a hand and mumble my apologies.

The makeshift brake wasn't very effective on icy downhills so when we came to a very tricky steep descent just before sundown, I suggested we 'chain up.'

I'd read in a gold rush era book by Arthur Walden called *A Dog Puncher on the Yukon* how dog team drivers had put chain under their toboggans or freight sleighs as a brake on steep hills. This appeared to be the ideal time to try, to save poor Tuk who had graduated from this morning's lead dog all the way back to wheel position. The big white Samoyed-cross was in real danger of being transformed into a small polar bear rug if Jan couldn't control the load on this particular icy hill.

Feeling rather smug for remembering this solution, I wrapped two dog chains around the curl of the toboggan and slid them down just under the front, into the snow.

"Now hold on tight and don't be afraid to tip the toboggan if the chains aren't enough," I instructed Jan. "We can't afford to carry any injured dogs. Especially a big fat one like Tuk."

She indicated her readiness, so I stepped around and skied off down the hill, calling Iskoot to follow. With the road so glazed from the day's thaw and freeze, I whooshed along at a terrifying clip, tucked down in a racing egg shape, coasting along the flat at the bottom, around the corner and down the next slope.

"Yahooooo!" I hollered and skated further on my skis, trees whizzing past and snow flying where my poles touched. Abruptly the forest opened to an incredible view of the Pelly valley and the setting sun. To my right was a large bare patch under a massive, old spruce, with plenty of standing firewood close by – perfect for tonight's camp.

But where were the dogs?

Maybe she dumped at the bottom of the hill, I worried, after waiting a few minutes, wondering if the toboggan would survive a high-speed impact. Or maybe she couldn't stop and has wiped out Tuk, I fretted as I started back up the slope. No, I'll bet she needed more chains to control the load properly and is putting on more. I skied faster, kicking hard to run up the hill, expecting to see them at the top of the rise, but— no one there…

Around the corner I raced, across the flat, but they weren't piled up at the bottom there either… I looked up, and finally spied them all – still at the very top, right where I'd left them!

When I arrived, breathless and sweaty, Jan was seated on the bank, eating snow and looking very annoyed once again. The dogs

The snow was too sticky to continue. The dogs sprawl in the snow with Rafferty staring very intently at the food Jan is unpacking.

were sitting or lying in their traces, and wagged tails happily at my arrival.

"Whatsamatter?" I panted.

"Won't move."

"Won't move?"

"That's what I said. Won't move."

"Oh."

So I pushed as hard as I could on the back of the load. It didn't budge an inch.

"See?"

"Yep. Won't move," I admitted.

So I pried up the front with a stout pole while Jan slid the chains off.

"I'll just use the brake," she said. "Okay?"

I wanted to explain that I really had read about using chains, but opted instead for mentioning the good camping spot half a mile ahead. Jan steered the toboggan there without any trouble or any more help from 'Mr. Bright Ideas' who sheepishly skied a respectable distance behind.

While unloading the toboggan, we let the dogs run loose for a moment. They suddenly came to life and bounded though the deep snow off the trail in pursuit of squirrels real and imaginary.

Rafferty didn't run with the rest but instead went under the tree where Jan was stretching out our sleeping bags and started to lift his leg—.

He was the first to get chained up, and when Tuk came back and wanted to rumble with Rafferty, I chained him, too. While I was there, the others returned and I fastened each to his own tree along the road with Mitti closest to our tree because she'd been the best behaved and could have the scraps from our meal. Soon each dog had dug or flattened a bed in the snow and was curled up, nose under tail, settled in for a snooze.

With the sun disappearing down the valley, the darkening sky became more noticeable – totally clear, warning of a cold night. A flicker of Northern Lights rippled across the heavens, entertaining us while we warmed our bones with soup and tea.

I melted a big panful of snow-water and cooked the dogs' supper a bit, a routine I'd been too tired to perform the night before. It was important, I'd been advised by 'real' mushers, to keep the dogs well hydrated. They gobbled it up, even Rafferty and Mitti, when I walked around in the moonlight and dished the glop out in the snow before each dog. Tuk was kicking up such a godawful racket that I fed him last, and almost lost my foot when he wolfed down everything within a twenty-inch radius of where I'd dumped his portion. He had the table manners or lack thereof of a Malamute; there was certainly no doubt about that side of his breeding.

Relaxing finally with our hot drinks, we stoked the fire to keep it from smoking too much and soon had a toasty bonfire. The flames began to lick the bottoms of socks drying on a rope over the fire so we pulled them to the side, and finally retreated ourselves as the heat increased to dry sauna intensity.

Jan was wearing her sunglasses, seeing if that would keep some of the smoke out of her eyes, and was obviously enjoying the kilocalories of energy engulfing her. Her blissed face was flushed in the intense heat as she squatted as close as possible to the blaze. The plastic sunglass lenses were also noticing the temperature, however. By the time Jan figured why the world was distorting like a Salvador Dali painting before her eyes, the lenses had inverted completely and were now concaved inwards! They were still wearable, she announced after a long silence, adding that they might even start a new fashion. I declined comment, not sure just how many calamities she could face in one day, and not wanting to push her over the edge with any well-meant teasing.

Later, as I was almost asleep, Jan returned from a last check on the dogs and a call-of-nature to report seeing two strange objects blink-blinking through the trees.

"Uh-huh," I murmured sceptically and sleepily. "Were you wearing your LSD sunglasses when you saw these lights?"

Jan didn't answer. From her silence I realized she had been quite serious about seeing some unidentified flying objects. Better just shut up, I realized.

Well, maybe they can help us get to Dawson, I mused and, comforted by that thought, soon fell asleep.

CHAPTER 5

PUSHING ONWARD

Morning.

I wiggled my toes and rubbed my feet together to get the blood circulating. There was a cool draft licking at the back of my neck where my toque didn't quite reach the collar of my sweater. My fingers were jammed into my armpits in search of heat.

Only my back was comfortably warm – even a little sweaty – where I was wedged tight against Jan. She was huddled, back towards me, wearing pale blue fuzzy pyjamas with attached feet, two sweaters and a toque.

Last night we'd zipped our sleeping bags together to share body heat, but had shared little else. Those flashes of smiles, the easy flirting, the hints of steamy romance that had punctuated our tavern room planning seemed long gone – dissipated in the stark reality of sweaty, smoky life on the trail. When Jan had said she felt too dirty even to be hugged, I didn't contradict her – we were both rank from all our exertions and darkened from hovering over cooking fires. Treat me like one of the boys, she insisted, and we'll just see how the trip develops. For some reason I hadn't felt hurt, or rejected – I was more focused on whether Jan was still willing to continue the trip. Without her help, could I make it to Dawson City?

Indeed, there may be no hope even with her best efforts, I thought, as we lay back-to-back, each shivering slightly. We hadn't yet seen the condition of the Yukon River ice. There would be a make-or-break, go-or-turn-back, possibly life-and-death decision to make over the next few days.

Slowly I opened an eye and looked out through the hoar frost ringing the mouth of the sleeping bag. The sky, I was pleased to discover, was covered in thick clouds. A high pressure front had moved in during the cold night, dropping the temperature to about 9°F and throwing an insulating blanket between the sun and our re-frozen trail.

Encouraged, I got up, kindled a fire and rearranged the clothesline, leaving Jan to nap a few minutes longer. Taking advantage of this private moment, I walked along the road and stood at a bend, staring out at the river valley beyond and below us. Apart from the dark green spruce, all was again those inimitable shades of gray: storm clouds overhead, rocky slopes cupping pockets of snow above a flat, wide river. The frozen Pelly, trackless and still, was like the flour-dusted floor of a timeless world. From this vantage point, the ice surface was almost smooth; yet I knew well that every slight wrinkle or scratch might actually be a five-foot-high pressure ridge.

We'd camped at the end of a long bench; from here the road descended further. I could see it strung out, carved out, even built out along the right river bank, a marvel of planning and engineering, delicately designed to require a minimum of bulldozer work to build and to maintain. The farmers had designed and constructed this road themselves as a 32-mile front laneway to move their beef out to market in the mining communities of the territory.

We'll make it easily to the Pelly Farm today, I thought. From summer canoe trips down both the Pelly and Yukon rivers, I was aware of three homes near the Pelly mouth. One was the farm – officially the Pelly River Ranch – on an ancient floodplain about fifteen miles travel from our present campsite. Next was John and Mickey Lammers' homestead a few miles further down on the opposite bank, and the third was Danny and Abby Roberts' small house in the Fort Selkirk townsite on the far, western bank of the Yukon River. Past these dwellings would be up to a hundred miles of wilderness travel before we'd meet up with the closest trappers who maintained a packed trail along the Yukon River to and from Dawson City.

Back under our camp-tree I added more snow to the tea billy. When Jan awoke, there were eggs and bread slices sizzling in the pan. For these first days we'd be eating the fresh and heavy foods, saving the dried staples, such as rice, oats, beans, raisins, noodles, flour and canned fish for the last leg. There was even peanut butter and cheese to spruce up the first days' snacks. Before leaving Whitehorse, we'd dried strips of beef from an 8-pound round roast – that was our emergency protein stash. Knowing that with so much exertion we'd crave carbohydrates, I'd made four loaves of very dense rye bread to eat on the first half of the trip. These loaves were baked in upright 48-ounce tin cans. After cooling, the bread had been packed in the same tin cans for protection. There were raisins and orange rind in the dough. After the loaves were consumed, we'd rely on the flour to make fried biscuit-like bannock.

"Whatcha thinking about?" I asked after breakfast was eaten in an uncomfortably long silence. "Worried about what's ahead?"

"More about what to do after we get there," she admitted. "I don't have rent money or enough for my truck payment. Don't know what I'll do. My work with the Follies doesn't start for another month, and it doesn't really pay much. I love it because everyone is so supportive – it's like a big family."

The Frantic Follies was a vaudeville show for the summer tourist trade. Jan, who'd grown up in Winnipeg and recently arrived in the territory, had been hired as a gaffer, ticket-taker and general odd-job person.

"Something will work out," I said. "Something always does. Have you got a long-term plan? Like what you want to do later, maybe in five years, or so?"

"You mean when I *grow up*?" she laughed. "Yeah, I've got a plan."

"And are you going to tell me? Or is it a secret? Promise I won't laugh. Really."

She took a deep breath and stared at me. The look said clearly, 'Don't you dare laugh.' Then she revealed that one day she would move to New York City or London and work for an art auction house. Sotheby's was the name she gave. In my ignorance, I'd never heard of it.

"Guess you know a lot about art," I said. "I'd never be able to live in New York. Just the thought of it gives me the creeps. Too crowded. Too busy. I'd feel lost. I'd go crazy within a day."

"I'd love it," Jan said, with confidence. "And to be surrounded by amazing art, and the people who understand it…" After a pause, she asked, "What about you? Going to be a hippie squatter forever until you move into an old folks home?"

"Maybe… not sure really. Guess I know more about the things I don't want to do – like work in an office or live in big city – than what I really do want." Looking around, I added, "Being in the Yukon bush is a wonderful place to be until I figure it out."

Jan stirred the fire and waited for me to continue.

"When my grade one teacher asked us what we wanted to be when we grew up," I said, "I didn't say a fireman or teacher or railroad engineer like the other kids."

"What did you say?"

" 'When I grow up, I'll be over six feet tall, like my dad.' Figure that gives me two inches of growing to do yet. Plenty of time left to figure out what to do, what my quest in life is."

She shook her head and smiled kindly. "Guess we'd better get this quest going then. It will be good to get to Dawson and have a bath."

By my pocket watch it was 11 o'clock when we finally slid away. The dogs were well rested and anxious to perform. I skied ahead, with Iskoot as lead dog hot on my trail – and tail. Literally. He wanted to walk on the back of my skis.

Tuk was at the very back, separated from Rafferty by the female Mitti plus Flander, who seemed too sneaky to get into a serious fight with big Tuk. Light-weight Casey was second, well away from Flander with whom he'd shared a few bites back at the highway. We thought we had them all figured out and geography would thwart their battle plans.

Near the foot of the longest incline, a cubic-foot-sized boulder had rolled into the centre of the road – easy to see and simple to avoid on skis. Over my shoulder I watched Iskoot and Casey step to the left, then Rafferty and Flander leap right over, with Mitti and Tuk veering left. The toboggan hit dead on. There was a resounding thud as wood crunched into stone – the boulder not budging an inch.

Jan had been standing – actually jumping – on the brake, which had little effect over the ice and gravel patches besides making lots of noise. Though she'd been somewhat braced for impact, the handlebars had smacked her hard in the ribs, leaving her gasping for breath. Shaking that off, she walked around to assess the damage and gave the boulder a push. When she couldn't move it, I offered to lend a hand. The boulder was frozen solid, virtually welded to the spot, so we backed the dogs up a bit and manoeuvred the toboggan sideways enough to slip past. Feeling the release of tension on their traces, the dogs suddenly bolted off, racing like all the demons of Hell were chasing them. Jan barely managed to grab on as the handlebars bounced past. She was jerked almost horizontal, her arms no doubt stretching six inches longer as she was dragged, struggling to gain a foothold on the toboggan. I scrambled to clip into my skis.

Only seconds later, Iskoot veered sharply off the road in pursuit of the squirrel he'd spotted, with the others following, rolling the toboggan on its side when it couldn't make the abrupt turn, and shearing Tuk's harness clips in the process. Jan somehow managed to step around and over the tumbling toboggan and wasn't hurt by the spill. Immediately I screamed at Iskoot to get back on the road but it was Casey who responded first, hauling Iskoot backwards and tangling Rafferty in his traces. With Rafferty hopping sideways like a solo three-legged racer, Tuk seized the opportunity to pounce, knocking Mitti onto Flander who yelped frantically. One yelp was all it took for Casey to loop back onto the pile, dragging Iskoot – now upside down and hog-tied in traces – who was snapping at any and every limb in sight. When Jan and I tried to pull the fighters apart, we became as tangled as they were, losing our footing in the deep snow and having to out-wrestle the most serious warriors.

Once again, after they had been stopped and each cautiously

unhooked and re-attached to the toboggan, the dogs began wagging tails as if to say that was grand fun, while Jan and I were left trembling and covered with snow and sweat.

"At this rate, we'll need ten years to reach Dawson, not ten days," I muttered, brushing snow off Jan's fanny.

"Maybe they'll work now that they've got that out of their system," Jan suggested hopefully. She pulled a length of poly rope from the repair stash and tied Tuk's traces directly to the toboggan, replacing the broken clips.

Her prediction proved surprisingly accurate. I continued skiing in lead, gradually paying less attention to the dogs behind and more to enjoying the forest ahead. Enormous snow flakes began drifting down gently and delicately, gracefully balancing on every twig and stalk of tall dried grass. Jan pulled on her canvas parka and had to run behind the toboggan to keep her feet warm. Hour after hour, she kept the dogs in line while the miles steadily passed under twenty-four furry feet. When the trail left the riverside, turning north toward the last creek crossing before the farm, the dogs were still pulling well and responding happily as Jan chattered and called out their names, addressing them like so many pre-schoolers on an outing to the zoo.

Twice I noticed leghold traps set beside the road, marked by an overhanging piece of fluorescent orange survey ribbon. Both traps had been sprung, one by an overly curious and now dead whiskey jack. We nonetheless hurried the dogs past the inviting bait, hoping they'd learn to avoid any future sets. Another advantage we had in our late season start was that trapping season was now officially closed. All traps were supposed to have been sprung five days earlier.

At the creek crossing, we had a welcome surprise. Here, where the flow usually freezes under the low log bridge and then glaciers up over the road into a 100-yard-wide barrier of flood water and thin ice, we encountered only a few wet patches to ford and piles of long, delicate ice candles to slalom a course through. The creek had obviously glaciered earlier but was now bubbling tamely beneath an icecap below the bridge.

"From here it is easy truckin' to the farm," I announced. "No more crossings!"

Jan cheered, Mitti barked and the others hung out purple tongues. As Jan pulled out the makings of a late lunch, I gave Iskoot a lecture on keeping the lines tight and not allowing the other dogs to get at each other. He acknowledged by rolling on his back and offering his tummy to scratch. Casey followed suit, wriggling snake-like on his back, inventing new knots with which to tangle the traces. When we sat down to eat our bread and sausage, they all sat up at attention in a line to offer paws, begging with pitiful eyes and drooling lips.

Jan volunteered to work the dogs again and I set the pace, having to double back to help right the toboggan only a few times. The dogs seemed to have found a rhythm and pulled willingly, although they never missed a chance to investigate the squirrels which chattered and screamed at us from the forest. Jan had Iskoot and Casey quickly trained to tighten up the line before she walked up to the front but, as there weren't any more fights, she let them get away with lots of short hold-ups to stare at screeching tree-dwellers. For my part, I was happier being away from the dogs, content for her to develop whatever style of mushing she wanted as long as it was getting us there.

The gently undulating plateau country with its relatively open deciduous forest had a relaxing, mesmerizing atmosphere. The steady flash-flash of sunlight through the poplars bordering this narrow lane could have been a hypnotist's metronome. I was almost asleep on my skis. Suddenly – breaking from the forest not 80 yards in front of me – a great ball of black-brown fur bounded across. Startled awake, I skied up to stare wistfully through the forest along the beast's path, hoping for one more glimpse… but it was gone. I crouched low to examine its tracks, but they weren't distinguishable at all. The thick snow crust had broken in icy chunks and plates, leaving only large dents and no detailed paw imprints. When Jan pulled up, six noses began working triple overtime, sniffing and sneezing frantically like a convention of hay fever sufferers. Our mystery animal was probably a wolverine – the most vicious of the forest carnivores – though these stout-bodied, razor-clawed predators reputedly prefer to travel at night. I'd never seen a wolverine before and certainly wouldn't want to spook one.

Coasting down the long straight stretch from the plateau was fun for me, but hair-raising for Jan. She came barrelling down the road, hopping on her virtually-ineffective brake and yelling commands that were largely ignored. We noticed a crudely-lettered sign nailed to a tree proclaiming we were *Entering Open Cattle Range* with a sketch of a rather jaunty bovine. To emphasize the point, horse and cow prints and manure began to appear on the road in increasing frequency. The dogs picked up the scents and their pace. On skis I could easily sidestep the frozen cow pies, but the dogs and toboggan just bounced over and onward, Jan still chattering to her charges and hanging on tightly. Soon the poplars yielded quick glimpses of the Pelly River, enormous and rough at such close quarters. Then the forest dwindled away, falling back to show us a half-section of flatland, walled to the north by steep hillsides and cut abruptly on the south border by the wide expanse of the Pelly. Across the river ice and past a few islands, cliffs rose sharply to define the width of the valley.

Brown dots low on the near slopes were cattle, searching out last year's dried grass where the snow had blown clear or melted off. In the first fields, we could see a few horses grazing on stubble poking through the snow. Ahead along the river bank was a cluster of log and board-sided buildings, their yards fenced with rough-milled planks, wood smoke spewing in low clouds from metal chimneys. The dull throbbing of a diesel generator and the barking of two loose dogs were the only sounds we could discern over the crunch and rasping of ice and gravel beneath our skis and toboggan.

But as I listened, there was another sound. It was the loud gasping of breath from sled dogs straining on their harnesses, tugging frantically forward, desperately eager to confront those two tail-wagging farm dogs. Iskoot and Casey lunged to pass me, sprinting towards their prey, with four more wide-eyed, tongue-flapping huskies thundering behind. I grabbed Rafferty's traces to hitch a wild ride and slow them slightly. At the last possible moment, I arrested their gallop by tripping a few dogs. Jan steered the toboggan deftly around us, barely managing to keep it upright as the traces tightened and spun it fully 180 degrees. Facing backwards, we'd made our arrival at the Pelly Farm.

"Whew!" I felt both relief and pride wash over me. We'd successfully completed the first test in our epic journey. Maybe we could pull off this quest after all.

CHAPTER 6

WELCOME

Greetings and gentle laughter floated down from the farmhouse doorway. Hugh Bradley, tall and lean, and dressed in grimy green coveralls, was in danger of losing the roll-your-own cigarette dangling from a grinning lower lip. Brother Dick peered over Hugh's shoulder, eyes twinkling as he stuffed his arms into the sleeves of a checkered wool bush shirt. In the window we could see Marjorie's round face pressed to the pane and young Glen's right beside her.

"Welcome, Bruce," Hugh called out. "That's quite an outfit you've got there!"

"Lots of raw power there, I imagine," Dick added as he followed Hugh across the yard to our gaggle of animals.

"Yeah, they're a bit too raw at times, Dick," I smiled. "But we'll get them cooking before long."

We shook hands and I introduced Jan. Hugh insisted on introductions to each dog as well, suggesting I do that while chaining them up to the fence near his cabin.

"Your timing is as good as ever, Bruce," Dick teased. "We were just having an afternoon break. I'll show Jan inside while you and Hugh tend to the dogs."

"Actually," Hugh smiled, "we'd finished our tea. But we don't mind doing it all over again, especially with entertainment. You can tell us what you're up to out here with all these sled dogs. I would have thought you'd be dusting off your canoe about now and getting ready for more river trips."

I could tell that my plans for an expedition down the Yukon River ice would be received with little enthusiasm by the farmers. It was, admittedly, very late in the season, and they'd had decades of experience living in the wilderness but, damn, I wanted to continue on.

At what point do caution and logic trump pride? Am I being too stubborn, I wondered as Hugh walked our lead dog by the collar through the barnyard. A hundred yards along the lane was the small, low log building where Hugh lived alone. We strung the dogs out, each chained to a fence post, and Hugh grabbed a pack from the toboggan.

"I take it you're staying for at least one night," Hugh said. "You can sleep in the upstairs of the farmhouse. You're welcome in my cabin, too, but it would be a bit crowded."

Once again, I found myself easily accepting the warm hospitality of the Pelly farmers. This was my third visit to the farm and on both summer visits I'd stayed far longer than planned, lulled by the relaxed farm pace and captivated by the stories and bush lore that accompanied every meal, chore and project. Both Dick and Hugh Bradley were great storytellers, needing only an interested audience. I was that eager listener, and eagerly joined in the farm work to earn my keep whenever I visited. The very existence of this beef farm – the most northerly working farm in

Canada – was amazing. It seemed so improbable to find a viable, fully fledged agricultural enterprise tucked away in this Yukon valley.

The farm was almost as old as the century, with the archaeological record indicating the site was used for many centuries, perhaps millennia, before as an Indian gathering spot. The two Lacombe, Alberta-raised Bradleys, along with an older brother, Ken, took over the farm in the early 1950s from the Wilkinson family who were using it mostly as a trapline headquarters. Since then, the Bradleys had experimented with a variety of livestock, deciding finally on a cow-calf operation, ranged during the warm weather and fed largely on Pelly Farm grain and silage over the winter. Hugh noted there were about fifty head of beef at peak times. If the crops didn't fare well during the summer, fewer cattle could be over-wintered and thus more meat would be marketed that fall. The years when crops did well were a chance to rebuild the herd's numbers.

The Bradley brothers were in their late 40s, wiry and well weathered.

Facing page: Pelly Farm, Hugh's cabin in foreground, farmhouse in background. Above: Hugh Bradley (left) and brother Dick Bradley.

They moved calmly, with purpose and a peaceful serenity that wouldn't have been out of place in a Buddhist monastery. Hugh pointed to a rusted tractor they'd been repairing that afternoon which could have been older than they were.

"We're not making a fortune," explained Hugh, "but this is what we like doing. That's why we're here."

Being where they are put the farm on many people's maps, with the accompanying advantages and disadvantages. Since the Canadian government closed its last northern agricultural research station at Haines Junction, the Bradleys had been testing new seed varieties for government scientists. Also, the certainty that someone was always going to be around to mind the animals had made the farm a secure, advance supply depot for surveyors, firefighters, miners and game wardens venturing into the region. A *National Geographic* article on the farm portrayed it as a noteworthy curiosity, though the resulting tourist numbers were mercifully minimized by the long, rough and dusty laneway. Even so, at times the procession of visitors expecting tea, guided tours and other assistance wore nerves thin, especially for the farm's sole female, Dick's wife Marjorie.

Back at the two-storey main farmhouse Marjorie told us she was already steeling herself for the summer, when at least one group of visitors drops in every day.

"Sometimes I feel I'm living in a museum!" she lamented, before adding quickly, "Thank God it was you, Bruce, coming today. You're hardly a tourist. You're more like someone else who lives in the bush. And we can always put you to work."

Jan was certainly being 'made useful', I noted. Marjorie had her preparing a pie for supper and was obviously relishing the female company. The two were talking up a storm in the kitchen.

Marjorie was telling Jan how she'd worked as a nurse in Ontario and met Dick through letters she'd helped an ailing old man write to the farmers. It must have taken remarkable courage for Marjorie, a single mom, to leave her southern roots four years ago and bring her young son to this so-remote corner of Canada, gambling their futures on a pen-pal romance.

I noticed young Glen Bradley at a small table in the living room, pretending to work at his correspondence school lessons. His ears were flapping, though, as he strained to catch every word said in the kitchen.

After spending every moment of the past two days outside, it felt strange being in a house again, complete with hot running water and electric lights. I felt protected, but somehow also cut off, from the elements. How easy it would be, I thought, glancing around the living room, to just give up on our trip and stay for a week in the comfort and security of the farm. So easy to be warm all day, and well fed five times a day. Yet for me the beauty of being in Nature depends very much on involving myself *fully*, actually being there totally, to acclimatize both my body and my mind. Whatever else it becomes, this trip would be an in-depth immersion in life outdoors.

During supper, Jan and I explained our plans. Hugh and Dick asked questions about the broken brake, the health of the dogs, distances and times we'd covered on the road in, the quantities of dog and people food we were carrying, whether we had a rifle [we didn't]; on and on as they tried to assess our chances of making it through to Dawson City.

"You may not find much ice on the Yukon River," Hugh said finally, and softly. "I'm not trying to discourage you or tell you what to do. What you do is completely up to you. And Jan."

He explained that Danny Roberts, when he came to the farm from Fort Selkirk for eggs on his snowmobile only a few days before, had reported a huge section of open water on the Yukon River in front of the old townsite and dangerous ice near the Pelly mouth. Danny was forced to go some miles upstream to find a safe route. We'd have Danny's trail across and down to Selkirk, but after that...

"Even when you get past that spot, Bruce," Dick continued, "there's another 180-odd miles of river. If you get into a stretch where the ice has jammed into blocks, you could be in for some pretty tough going, manoeuvring a team and toboggan through and over and around. Even the Cowboy tried it one year and had to turn back."

The cowboy Dick was referring to was Larry 'Cowboy' Smith, almost a legendary figure in the Yukon, renowned for his tenacity and determination. Smith now trapped 60 miles down the Yukon at Coffee Creek, but had previously spent winters trapping and training sled dogs in this Pelly-Yukon confluence area. To hear that Smith had tried to force his way down the river from Selkirk to meet the packed trails out of Dawson and been forced back by deep snow and almost impenetrable ice pile-ups was quite disheartening. Although single-handed, he would have had a crackerjack team and no urgency about warm weather.

"I still want to give it a try," I said, feeling somewhat embarrassed. "Maybe we won't get through. But maybe we will."

I glanced across at Jan, who was listening intently to every word but remaining silent. If she'd made a decision about turning back, she wasn't voicing it now.

"It must have been hard work for the dog teams that ran the mail route from Whitehorse to Dawson," I offered, "and somehow they got through. I'm sure there were some well-travelled sections near the settlements but they'd still have to break trail after storms and make their way through rough areas like we're facing – wouldn't they, Hugh?"

Hugh paused, licked his lower lip and then grinned.

"Sure, Bruce, I understand the dog teams made it through for the years when they were used. At least, I never read where they didn't..." He paused again. "But dogs weren't used to move the mail for very long over this route. The mail and passengers were taken by horse-drawn sleigh and stage coach as soon as the overland trail was built, a few years after the gold rush of '98."

My mind was whirling: What? Where was this overland trail and what's it like today? Could this be our route to Dawson if the Yukon River ice was impassable? Hugh and Dick were glancing back and forth, realizing that I hadn't known about a stage route paralleling the river.

"Maybe I better get out a map," Dick said, slipping away from the table.

"And maybe we'll need another pot of tea," Hugh said with a grin. "I never figured you didn't know about the old stage road, Bruce. I just thought you had your mind set on travelling the river."

For two hours we poured over topographical maps of the area, with the farmers pointing to tiny dashes that snaked over the contour lines, branching and joining in a web of ancient trails and paths. The stage road's right-of-way actually defined the western boundary of the farm property. From here, the route followed one creek for a stretch, then crossed to another, then another. If we went this way we'd be navigating largely by watersheds. Hugh pencilled in local names to several anonymous thin blue lines: Horsefell Creek, Black Creek, Jane Creek and so on over to Scroggie Creek, which flowed into the Stewart River. From there we could either head down the Stewart ice to the Yukon River – where we'd be certain to pick up packed snowmobile trails to Dawson – or instead cross the Stewart and continue on the overland route until we would be on the mining roads south-east of Dawson. I pumped Dick and Hugh for every detail but neither of them had been all the way across to the Stewart. They did tell me that Peter Isaac, an Indian living in Pelly Crossing, had trapped along the stage road this past winter, ensuring us a packed snowmachine trail for at least part of the way.

It was after midnight when Dick went out to shut off the diesel generator. A chorus of barking signalled that all was not right in the dog lot, so I threw on my parka and ran over with a flashlight to see what was up. Snowflakes swirled in the yellow beam, the prelude to a blizzard, I was sure, and the temperature was dropping quickly. Already a half-inch of new snow had smoothed the cow prints around the barn. Tuk was on his feet, barking indignantly and looking further down the fence. Rafferty, his rival, had broken his tether and was curled up over against Flander.

In the glare, their eyes shone red like a demon's, but both Tapsell dogs wagged tails slowly and yawned like sleepy angels while I wired a new snap on Rafferty's chain. I refastened his chain to the adjacent fencepost so Rafferty wouldn't need to break free to be near his buddy. A fluffy white blanket had drifted over Mitti and Casey and Iskoot where they lay curled in tight balls, not moving at my passing.

For a moment I stood in the wind, staring at the dim, ghostly outline of the Pelly River and breathing deeply. The cold air tickled the hair in my nostrils and tingled in my lungs. A sudden shiver ran down my spine.

Tomorrow we'd test that Pelly ice, exploring down to the Yukon River. There we'd make our choice of routes to the Klondike.

Better give up on this whole idea before it is too late, counselled the voices. *So irresponsible.*

"Oh, shaddup," I muttered aloud and walked past the dogs to the farmhouse, kicking up the loose snow ahead of me with each defiant step.

CHAPTER 7

CROSSING THE YUKON RIVER

Hugh Bradley rummaged through a pile of old planks and plywood pieces, all carefully stored away 'just in case.' As each board was disturbed, a puff of coarse saw-dust and fine, brown Pelly River silt billowed upwards. Morning sunlight, squeezing through cracks in the board-and-batten shed walls, illuminated thin sparkling wedges of air. I could certainly smell the dust, but there was also a lingering odour of chicken manure – perhaps clinging to my boots from a pre-breakfast visit into the hen house to gather eggs.

"We've certainly got just what you need," Hugh drawled. "It's just a matter of finding it."

Living so far away from a town and stores made necessary a pack rat-like hoarding of odds and ends, and the conservation of any supplies bought 'outside.' Although the farmers milled their own pine, spruce, and occasionally birch or poplar lumber, Hugh was searching for a stronger material.

"This should do 'er," he said finally, pulling out a short plank and passing it across the pile to me. "I'm not exactly sure what wood that is, but it is some southern hardwood. And I'll bet even you can't break it."

The inch-thick plank had considerable heft and, I soon discovered, was difficult to auger bolt holes through. Sawing off a foot-long section with a dull hand saw was taking so long that Hugh fired up the diesel generator – usually not turned on until noon – and plugged in an electric circular saw. Moments later we bolted on the angle iron teeth and installed the new brake pad on the back of our toboggan.

"Come to think of it," Hugh stated with mock seriousness, "it looks like you won't break this board but will be able to brake *with* it."

"Very punny, Hugh," I acknowledged. "And thanks yet again for coming to my rescue."

"Happy to help out. I'm glad you'll have some snow for that brake to bite into."

Last night's storm had given us an additional two-inch cushion over the ground – and over the ice. Though the sun was shining now, the occasional large flake was drifting down from the dark clouds crowding in from the west. No doubt we'd be mushing through a building storm to reach Fort Selkirk today.

Right after lunch, with the dogs all harnessed and eager, and good-byes said, we were about to pull away when a snowmachine towing a metal sled roared past us, swerving wide to miss the dogs, and stopped in front of the farmhouse.

"Peter Isaac," I answered Jan's raised eyebrows. "He must be coming out from his trapline on the old stage road, heading for Pelly Crossing. I'll go ask him about the trail."

Our timing is awesome, I thought as I hurried over. Leaving two minutes earlier, we'd have missed him.

Peter talked to Dick, Hugh and me in the slow cautious manner so typical of those who live for weeks without talking to anyone. He was helpful and, I felt, even encouraging. Yes, there was lots of snow on the trail, especially in the hills. No, there weren't any really tricky spots – his packed trail looped through the lower Horsefell and Black Creek areas, but rejoined the stage road after his Black Creek line cabin.

"All my traps are sprung," he said in a very soft, calm voice, "so you don't have to worry about your lead dog. And there is lynx meat at one of the cabins you can feed them if you want."

When I attempted to confirm the exact cabin locations on the map, Peter became rather ill-at-ease. Though the slight Pelly Crossing Indian knew this entire area better than most southerners know their own homes, topographic maps appeared to confuse rather than clarify matters. In a sudden move, Peter whirled away and began fishing through a canvas bag on the metal sled. Then, with a triumphant grin, he handed me a packet of photographs: shots of line cabins, captured animals, furs on stretcher boards, even a few of Christmas parties in Pelly Crossing.

Jan had now joined us and Dick suggested we all go inside for tea. But before we made a step towards the door, we were interrupted by a commotion coming from near Hugh's cabin. Although we sprinted, the dogs were hard at it before we arrived. Iskoot was fighting with Flander while Rafferty and Tuk had resumed their grudge match. The first event seemed to have done little harm except breaking Casey's harness where Jan had just mended it, but Tuk was cut and bleeding above his eye. An inch lower might have meant a lost eye but Tuk didn't seem to grasp the seriousness of scrapping. He was panting vigorously, lurching at his restraints, ready for more.

"Why wasn't Iskoot chained?" I asked Jan, none too politely. Tying the lead dog against the fence should have kept the dogs in line, unable to fight.

Jan didn't answer. She'd realized her mistake and kept her back to me while she clipped on the cross-country skis. "Give me a good head start," she muttered finally, "and keep Iskoot from walking on the back of my damn skis—."

She didn't add 'you asshole' but clearly was thinking it.

Well, I sure didn't handle *that* very well, I thought and shook my head.

Watching her silhouette slide away down the farm lane, slowly shrinking in size as the minutes ticked away, was altogether too much for the dogs to bear. While I retied his harness, Casey started leaping high into the air, making pained squealing noises. Mitti began barking frantically. Tuk pawed at the snow. Iskoot tugged in his traces, and Rafferty chewed on his. Flander moaned pitifully and looked over his shoulder pleadingly at me. Despite my commands to 'sit' and 'stay,' the team repeatedly attempted to jerk the toboggan into motion. Our newly repaired brake would hardly have slowed such determination – I had the toboggan's trailing gee-line tied securely to a tree to ensure against a false start. I waited a full five minutes before silently slipping the knot.

I waved goodbye to Dick, Hugh and Peter. Then, with surely the quietest "Okay, let's go!" command I've ever given, we were off at a full gallop, bouncing down the rutted lane, heading southwest into the sun's glare. A few flurries were drifting down but the clouds hadn't yet succeeded in fully blocking the sky. The dogs had spirit and enthusiasm to burn, rushing me to the end of the farm lane where I quickly glanced right, northward up Peter Isaac's snowmachine trail on the old stage road. Jan's ski tracks in the fresh snow abruptly plunged left, down over the river bank, taking us way out on the Pelly River ice. Here the river had frozen almost glassy-smooth, like a quarter-mile wide outdoor skating rink coated with maybe four inches of snow. Quickly we rushed by an island, the skis' imprints faithfully leading us along Danny Roberts' skidoo track. Moments after the dogs caught sight of Jan's figure out ahead of us, we were full-galloping again, closing the distance in a delightful rush. Then, with 14 eyes watching, she suddenly toppled over into a snow drift.

We raced up to find her lying on her back, making a snow angel outline with her arms and grinning happily. Iskoot never lost a step and jumped right on top, leading the team in a merry pile-up-on-Jan. She laughed and wrestled with them, rubbing snow in their faces and rolling them in the loose snow. The wheel dogs, who couldn't quite get into the action, wagged their tails heartily. Mitti, of course, barked manically throughout the excitement.

For the moment it was hard to imagine these silly animals as anything but a big happy family of pets. They were equally ready to work or to play, and full of love for Jan.

While she skied ahead, I had no discipline problems, indeed little to do except the task of holding them back off her heels. I hopped on the brake and stage-whispered, "Slowly, slowly," to hold Iskoot back.

To our right a sheer, 500-foot cliff of basalt rock loomed over us. At this point, where the edge of the volcanic plateau funnelled the river against a 3,100-foot mountain on the left shore, the swift current had frozen in a fury of tumbled ice. We followed Danny's course, threading our way through the monster blocks of ice and haphazard drifts of snow. Sheets of ice as big as a suburban house lot had lifted and tilted wildly, exposing a thickness of over four feet of solid ice.

If one or two inches will support a person's weight, I rationalized to myself, there should be plenty to carry us almost anywhere on the Yukon. It was hard to believe four feet had formed here and there'd be none somewhere close by.

The Pelly was now pointing almost due south, making its final grand sweep into the Yukon's wide valley. We mushed around the shoulder of the sentry mountain and pulled up below a cluster of low frame buildings high up on the eastern bank. This was the year-round home of John and Mickey Lammers, who operated an eco-tourist guiding business from this retreat in the wilderness. Visitors from the States and Europe were escorted on canoe trips down a variety of Yukon rivers. The only shooting was with cameras. Jan had met the Lammers in Whitehorse and scrambled up the slope to say hello while I waited with the team. The dogs grabbed an opportunity to nap, digging and compacting snow nests before curling nose-under-tail. I was settling in for a few Zs myself when Jan called down that I should come up to have tea.

"We've got lots of time to reach Fort Selkirk before dark, don't we?" she shouted.

"We'll be fine as long as we can wake the dogs!" I laughed. After tying the gee-line back to a tree and roping Iskoot ahead to a driftwood log, I joined Jan and Mickey in the toasty warmth of the main cabin. John was away in Whitehorse tending to guest bookings for the upcoming season, we learned, and was due back tonight. His route out to the main highway was actually via the southern continuation of the old overland stage road. The right-of-way passed through the Lammers property. Heading towards Whitehorse, it hugged the mountain, climbed into the rolling country behind Minto Flats and eventually merged with the all-weather Klondike Highway. In the other direction, toward Dawson, the route held tight to the near shore around the foot of the mountain until crossing the river just below the farm.

We chatted about chinking cabin logs, garden fertilizers and temperature controls on wood stoves until we'd eaten all of Mickey's goodies and emptied the tea pot twice.

As we roused the dogs and knocked the snow off the skis, Mickey asked which colour ski wax Jan was using. I flipped over a ski to show Mickey the gouged, bare birch base; she was clearly aghast at the sight. "Oh," was all she could manage.

"Every type of wax I've tried wears off almost immediately on the ice lumps and spring snow crust," I explained, "even klisters. Even pine tar wears off in a few hours."

Hurrying through our journey, we were completely ignoring the customary rituals of propane mini-torch, sticks of wax, tubes of gooey klister, cloth rags, cork pads and metal scrapers. As Jan skied away down the river, Mickey Lammers' raised eyebrows underlined her assessment that Jan was learning very poor habits and developing improper technique. To compensate for the lack of grip-and-glide wax or klister, Jan was using far more arm action than was 'proper'; she moved in an exaggerated slide-shuffle with her arms pumping like pistons. Still, despite her questionable style, Jan was setting a fair pace and was almost out of sight down the first slough channel. I shrugged my shoulders, waved thanks to Mickey, and called on Iskoot to "Go get her."

From the Lammers' place, Danny's winter route to Selkirk was normally around six miles; this year's version was about ten. His trail took us down narrow backwater channels, across gravel bars barely covered with snow and over low marshy flats. When we could clearly see the confluence of these two mighty rivers, I pointed out Fort Selkirk in the distance, across two miles of ice and a sinister dark streak of open water. The tiny shapes of buildings were barely discernible from here but I was encouraged to have tonight's destination in sight.

The on-again, off-again snowfall was definitely on-again now, spilling large wet flakes from the gun-metal skies. The wind was picking up, too, as we made our way south, up the Yukon River and away from the confluence. Danny had kept mostly to the thick shelf ice against the east shore, motoring two miles upstream before crossing the Yukon through a maze of islands and sloughs. To cross one island, he'd axed a trail for a quarter of a mile through thick willows, an exhausting chore he certainly wouldn't have undertaken if he had believed there was safe ice over any alternative. Other island detours took us through patches of second-growth spruce, where we ducked overhanging branches and leaning deadfalls and were chided by indignant squirrels.

The temperature kept plunging. To keep warm on the back of the toboggan, I layered on more clothes and stomped my feet.

Jan's energy was waning and the new snow was clumping under those long wooden feet. The dogs, too, were losing interest and baulking when extra muscle was required on the cross-island detours. Rather than feel frustrated by the slow progress, I elected to trade places with Jan and burn off a little energy myself.

After a half-mile crossing of the main channel – Danny's route was quite straight here – we were finally at the western shore of the Yukon River. The trail immediately mounted the steep bank and headed off into the forest. I ran up the grade, pushing hard on my poles to reach the lip before my forward momentum petered out. Looking back from the top, I could see the dogs hadn't made it onto the slope at all. The toboggan had caught on a protruding branch at the shoreline and tipped on the ice.

I unclipped the skis and ran back to help Jan who was wading around in the deep snow beside the snowmobile trail turning the air blue with her thoughts.

"How come you always ski on the easy parts?" she demanded and glared at me.

The toboggan was wedged firmly between branches and it took all our combined strength to lift it up onto the packed trail again. Then I walked ahead and pulled the dogs forward, holding Iskoot's collar and heaving on his traces; Jan pushed and strained at the back of the toboggan. Sweat was flowing from my armpits – the droplets trickled cold down my ribs. Glancing over my shoulder, still straining with my legs to inch the load up the bank, I was shocked to see four tails up and wagging gaily in the air! Working with sled dogs can be so very frustrating at times, and unfortunately when the musher over-reacts, the situation typically gets worse, not better. I knew that, yet I boxed ears with my leather mitts anyway and yelled at them until all the crew at least kept their tails low and pretended to work. Finally we muscled our way up the bank, but no one was feeling at all cordial.

On the flat now, I clipped on the skis again and hurried ahead, not really wanting to be near the dogs – nor to Jan's mood. Fuelled by the storm inside me, I raced through the birch and poplar forest, straining to skate as fast as I possibly could, stomping my skis intermittently to dislodge the snow caking on the base. The river occasionally appeared through the trees to our right, showing off its chaotically jammed ice. I pushed onwards, stopping only to shed my jacket and then my sweater, too, as I heated up. Gigantic flakes were landing on my vest, then slowly melting in the heat being released through the down insulation. Other flakes were lodging on my eyelashes or splattering on my forehead. It's rather hard to take yourself too seriously with snow on your face. I was beginning to get my humour back.

Whether the dogs were sensing Jan's no-nonsense mood or just enjoying biting at snowflakes, they kept within fifty yards of me, trotting without incident for miles as the forest gradually petered out. Abruptly we found ourselves mushing down a long corridor of snow-draped, dilapidated wooden buildings. This collection of log and plank skeletons, the once-proud headquarters of the Yukon Field Force, was a jolting respite after the stormy crossing. The townsite was another major milestone. From here it was about 180 miles of river travelling to Dawson City. I could feel the clouds of frustration dissipating inside me and sunshine breaking through. We'd reached old Fort Selkirk!

Jan and I exchanged tired smiles. The dogs wagged their tails tentatively.

CHAPTER 8

FORT SELKIRK

Although I'd been to old Fort Selkirk by canoe before, it took a few moments to orient myself. The ghost town stretches along a sandy bluff overlooking the broad Yukon River. Abandoned parade grounds and army buildings, those shells we passed first on our arrival, form the south-east edge of town. The former military encampment is about a mile downstream and a full mile across the Yukon River from the mouth of the Pelly. In 1898, when tens of thousands of gold seekers from all over the world stampeded to the Klondike Hills near Dawson City, an armed presence was established in the Yukon to ensure order and maintain Canadian sovereignty in the face of potential U.S.-Canada boundary disputes. The Yukon Field Force made its headquarters here on the site of an 1848 Hudson's Bay Company fur-trading post – the original Fort Selkirk. I tried to imagine armed sentries and saluting soldiers as they would have greeted an in-coming dog team carrying the mail and other news during winters at the turn of the century. Or the half-starved (typically Scots descent) fur traders of 50 years earlier exuberantly welcoming a supply sled and instructions from their company superiors (the self-styled 'gentlemen adventurers') back in London, England.

Beyond the parade square, we came to the stores, school, churches, telegraph office and houses of a once-thriving town, looking now like a Hollywood film lot, ready for cameras to roll on a snowy spaghetti western. This settlement had flourished during the gold rush and afterwards, serving as a supply centre for the immediate area. But in the 1950s when an all-weather highway was built to connect the Keno-Elsa silver mines (and Dawson City) with Whitehorse's railway connection to the coast, the town's economy was devastated. The picturesque sternwheelers that plied the Yukon River soon lost their freight and passenger contracts and, one by one, they were beached. In a few short years, Fort Selkirk essentially became obsolete – a river port with no boat traffic.

The Indian peoples who comprised much of Selkirk's population had been supplementing their meagre trapping incomes (for fur prices were low in those years) by cutting cordwood for the riverboats' boilers. With the boats retired, most families moved to a traditional village upstream at Minto Landing, close to the new highway. In the 1960s when a store and school were built near the bridge crossing the Pelly, people relocated to this new settlement. For ease of administration, government Indian Agents pressured any hold-outs at Selkirk and Minto to move also to Pelly Crossing. There, a pattern of doling out welfare payments became a ritual, an institution. The children were educated in schools where the self-righteously proclaimed mandate was to turn the young heathen savages into good God-fearing Christians who spoke only English and would lose their 'inferior' native culture. With poor employment opportunities, their families rent apart and little self-esteem, many adults became depressed and turned to booze. Some chose suicide. It had taken much time, courage and determination for the Pelly Crossing community to begin turning itself around.

One Indian couple, Danny and Abby Roberts, missed the last major exodus from Fort Selkirk when they were downriver trapping. They returned to find the town almost vacant. Within a year, their two remaining neighbours also departed. Danny shrugged his shoulders and started trapping with his dog team right from the town itself. His wife Abby raised a baby girl and managed her own dog team. Except for a few seasons away for health reasons or for construction work, they'd lived in the old town ever since, chasing bears and tourists out of the buildings, and listening to the CBC's Wee Willie Anderson country music show on a crackling radio during the long winter nights.

We came within 100 feet of their cabin under the cover of the thickening snowfall before Danny's tethered dogs scented or heard us and sounded the alarm. Danny poked his head out the door, nodded at our "Hello!" and ducked back inside. I skied over to their modest cabin – certainly one of the smallest buildings in the town – while Jan stopped the dogs and told each in turn to sit.

In a moment Danny, wearing his captain's hat, re-emerged to chat. He recognized me from summer canoe trips, laughing as he spotted Casey: "You still got that orange dog!" He asked which way we'd come and inquired if we wanted to stay in the 'tourist cabin.' I complimented Danny on his trail from the Pelly, learning that it had taken him two days to scout all the channels and clear the way across some of the islands. Much as I wanted to talk on, we were all getting wet standing there, so we accepted his offer of lodging and said goodbye until morning.

The tourist cabin was the only new building in Fort Selkirk, located past all the other structures at the northern (downstream) edge of town in

Danny Roberts, trapper, fisherman and caretaker of the Fort Selkirk historical site, wearing his signature captain's hat.

a camping area set aside for canoeists' use in summer. We were delighted to find a pile of split wood beside the cabin door and a cast iron Fisher wood heater inside. Jan unloaded kitchen gear and lit the fire while I found fence posts to chain the dogs to, with Rafferty and Tuk at opposite sides of the cabin so they couldn't see one another and moan and growl all night. Soon we had the cabin bright with candles, and clothes steaming on various ropes strung out behind the stove. The first supper prepared was a roasting pan full of snow-water and dogmeal so our boys (and girl) could enjoy a hot meal. Jan was the heroine of their hearts for dishing out four steaming, smelly cupfuls each, poured in the snow beside their nests. Though they were essentially being served supper-in-bed, no gentility was displayed. Instead they each put on an appalling, four-legged roaring vacuum cleaner impersonation. Tuk, waiting frantically for his ration to be served, wailed like a keener at an Irish wake, no doubt clearing the town of all but the deafest of ghosts. There was something in him that shut off his brain whenever food was present. To teach him a poodle trick such as balancing a biscuit on his nose would have required chain-mail gauntlets.

The dog-feeding chore completed, we prepared soup and sandwiches for ourselves and settled down to an evening in our sleeping bags, reading by candlelight. A tired Jan managed all of two pages before dozing off, but I persisted through a couple of chapters of my spy novel. After half an hour, Danny's dogs began howling mournfully and ours joined in. I glanced up from the pages, noticing the flickering candles reflecting on the window panes and dancing shadows from our hanging clothes. Here in this cabin was the spooky atmosphere my author had vainly spent thousands of words trying to create. I blew out the lights and snuggled deep into my bag.

I lay there for a few more moments, debating our course onwards to Dawson as all-too-vivid images appeared, sending chills down my spine: I could clearly see the pristine Yukon River ice, blinding white in the afternoon sun, and across it was a black gaping wound, oozing and flowing with frothy, frigid, blood-thick water. Then the current became a gigantic, slimy reptile, ever rolling and grasping and clawing away at the fragile translucent shell above it. On the river were two miniature people and six tiny dogs, moving slowly, unaware the ice ahead of them was being gnawed away from underneath. There were paper-thin patches certain to break as soon as the people stepped on them; the dark cold creature was waiting below. I sat up quickly and opened my eyes, desperate to chase the visions away, to shake everything from my mind.

In the near-dark, I recognized the humped shape of Jan's sleeping form and felt a bit less panicky. From inside me came the grim realization of how afraid I had really been out on the ice today, how the constant terror of falling through was eating away inside me. Jan and I had agreed to wait and consult with Danny in the morning about our choices, but my subconscious mind was clearly working on a course all its own.

I glanced again at my sleeping partner and wondered how I would have managed without her. But the question was rather rhetorical for deep down I knew the answer. Alone I would had been hard-pressed to drive these undisciplined dogs even this far. Without her participation, there would be no trip to Dawson City.

At first light I was up and busy. I dragged the toboggan inside and inverted it on the table so all the bolts and screws could be tightened. Next the ropes were re-laced, tightened, repaired where worn, or replaced. A thick layer of candle wax seemed to evaporate right into the shaggy, scarred base. Waiting for that to dry, I hauled in all the harnessing and other equipment, spreading it out until the cabin was covered in half-sorted, half-finished projects and repairs, with puddles of melting snow in every corner and leather traces draped from every nail on every wall. When Jan woke, she had a glass of Scotch and a Rothman's and wrote in her diary with a double-ended silver-and-red pencil Glen Bradley had given her. It said Alberta Wheat Pool on the side.

I opened a can of herrings in tomato sauce and – ever one to experiment – served them beside pancakes made using the leftover soup for the liquid. It wasn't one of my better breakfasts.

For a second batch, the batter was much thicker, forming biscuit-like cakes that locals call *bannock*, I explained to Jan. We were using baking powder in our doughy batter; pioneers used yeast to make their biscuits rise. You can bake the dough in an oven, even wrap it around a stick and roast it over a fire.

Tummies full, we fled with Jan's camera to explore the town and visit its only residents.

The Anglican Church at Selkirk inspired us with its precise woodworking and delicate design. We carefully set up slow speed exposure shots of the light streaming through the coloured glass onto the fine panelled walls. A Bible lay photogenically open on the pulpit.

"I think He would have liked this place," Jan said in a reverent whisper. "It's His birthday today, you know."

"Christ's birthday in April?"

"No, not Jesus. It's Buddha's birthday today."

As we continued through the town toward Danny's, we could hear the river roaring ominously below and see the black swirling waters. Huge cakes of ice floated along the open channel like so many ice cubes until they smashed into the pile-up at the end. There, these massive cakes thrashed about until they were either jammed fast into the heap or drawn down under the ice surface by the powerful current. A person afloat in that water would have no chance of surviving. I was glad we had another option for travel – at least as far as the Stewart River.

Danny and Abby greeted us warmly and stood with us in the 40°F sun. Selkirk, who was Abby's 17-year-old retired lead dog, struggled to his feet and woofed in our general direction. Behind him, his son and two other long-legged monsters paced back and forth, racing to the ends of their chains' reach, constantly in motion, bodies turning but never taking their eyes off us. The ground at their chain perimeters was deeply rutted from their perpetual pacing. As we watched, one dog strutted into his dog house and right back out, never missing a step and never looking away. They were a study in hyperactivity, hybrid sled dogs bursting with raw instinct and energy. These mongrels were taller than Tuk and Rafferty and looked as though they could easily eat either of them for lunch. No one could possibly confuse these wolf-like, wild-eyed creatures with half-pet huskies like ours. We didn't dare stand too close.

Danny told us the two tall dogs were cast-offs from Cowboy Smith's team, which brought the topic around to the question of following the river ice to Dawson.

"Could be pretty tough," Danny offered quietly.

Abby said nothing.

"Maybe you won't make it. Maybe you'll have to make a camp and wait on shore for break-up. Then you make a raft and go down that way. Have you got a rifle to get some meat?"

Abby still was silent, blinking in the sunshine. Then she abruptly turned back into their cabin, muttering loudly, "You're crazy to do that. But it's not my business. I'm going to get a smoke."

Jan, who liked the occasional cigarette, followed Abby inside. Danny and I soon crowded into the small cabin, too, in search of tea and a snack.

Their home was no more than 16 x 12 feet. Danny had built it with roughly milled plank walls and cardboard for insulation. Only its diminutive size made it practical to heat through a Yukon's fierce winter – and today it was stifling hot as a wood stove roared to boil tea water. Abby sat on the low bed, playing with her pet dog, Timmy, a tiny Heinz 57 lap dog with a poodle's quick, yappy bark. "This is my baby," she said, then added brightly, "Did you know I'm a real grandmother now?"

Danny giggled at the thought and told us that their own marriage had been unpopular because it went against the traditional moiety rules. They were both from the same clan, the Crows, and weren't supposed to intermarry. Their daughter and her child lived in Pelly Crossing. As we chattered on together, Jan and Abby puffed away merrily until the front room was blue with smoke. Danny suddenly convulsed into a coughing fit and struggled out the door, his face dark and gasping for fresh air. Abby looked at him disdainfully and turned to Jan.

"Gees, it sure bugs me when he do that," she said. "It ruins a good smoke!"

Danny and I walked around outside for a while and he showed me the new sled he had just built for towing behind his 'white man dog team' as he calls his Skidoo snowmachine. This new plywood sled was wider – 26 inches – so Abby could sit in it more comfortably. They were, in fact, planning to try this sled for the first time tomorrow on a last quick trip into Pelly Crossing before break-up. On the underside, overlapped sheets of galvanized metal covered the base.

"In the winter, when it's really cold, a wood toboggan slides good. Now in the spring, metal works not too bad. On a dog toboggan it's better to have some runners, so you don't wear out the bottom on the ice and snow crust," he explained, pointing to two rusted iron strips leaning against a shed wall. "Those were the type they used on the freight sleighs back in the old days."

Each was perhaps eight feet long, with bolt holes every foot or so. I hefted one and estimated it weighed at least 15 pounds. Danny had made his old dog toboggan from local birch, though many mushers used oak planks the trading company imported from southern Canada. Each type of wood was best for a certain temperature range, Danny said, though he had no idea about our possibly-ash base.

Brakes on toboggans were a fairly recent development. Danny remembered many teams with very many Indian families arriving for a potlatch ceremony long ago and that had been the first time they had put brakes on their toboggans. "Before that, the wheel dog he had to be pretty quick to get out of the way sometimes!"

Danny so casually and happily talked about trapping, cutting cordword, running a dog team – not just living in the bush but *thriving* there. His earlier remark flashed back, about us maybe needing to make a camp and waiting for break-up. No doubt Danny could camp for months without a problem and would probably even come out with a huge cache of fish, beaver, bear and moose meat. But I couldn't do that. Someday, maybe, but not with my current knowledge and capabilities, not by a long shot.

Both Jan and I were so enjoying being with Danny and Abby and hearing about the 'old times' that I ducked back inside to hold a quick conference with Jan. We quickly agreed to stay on until tomorrow, giving us a chance to rest thoroughly and also to entertain our hosts with a supper in the tourist cabin. Abby's face burst into a big smile when we mentioned that she was "invited for a night out on the town." Many years had passed since they'd had winter neighbours.

Jan dug deep into the grub box to assemble a 'fancy dinner'. We fried up sausages to accompany a package of frozen green beans. A package of freeze-dried potatoes was transformed into 'mushroom scalloped spuds à la Selkirk', and a tin of fruit cocktail was thawing for dessert. Our remaining mickey of Lamb's Navy Rum would serve as the apéritif.

Danny drove over on his motorized 'yellow dog team,' towing Abby in her new sled. I'm not sure who enjoyed the evening more but at times I had the feeling that there were a few extra residents of this ghost town in attendance, charging the air with light energies and conjuring some of Fort Selkirk's past hospitality. The rum disappeared awfully fast.

While exploring the town earlier, Jan and I had visited the one-room schoolhouse, and we now asked what it had been like to grow up in Selkirk.

"I sat at the back, near the door," Danny laughed. "And I didn't go many years before I started to work, cutting wood for the steamboats."

Abby's story was quite different. She was younger than Danny and had grown up under a different system. At seven she was separated from her family and shipped away to the Carcross Mission School and forced to speak only English. "They beat us if we spoke our Indian language and I forgot it all. When I came back, I couldn't even talk to my own grandmother anymore. I couldn't speak Indian anymore."

But she persisted and learned the 'Indian Ways' from the elders so she could now use some of the herbal medicines to cure colds and coughs. "We didn't learn by schools, or books, or by television like they've got in Pelly Crossing. We learned from our parents and grandparents. Even sometimes there was a potlatch just to show people things and how to do something. I helped and watched the old people. I learned the Indian ways. That's how you learn – not by asking stupid questions all the time."

The rum was making Abby rather morose – albeit yes, I had been asking questions virtually non-stop all day. Every little thing they had said I wished could be preserved, not just for the information, but also for the poetry and music in their voices. With Abby's dark brown eyes piercing and searching me from behind her glasses and Danny's quite-oriental eyelids winking his thoughts, the conversation finally turned to Jan and me and our trip.

"Maybe you'll have no toboggan left by the time you reach Stewart," Danny pointed out softly. "The bottom wears out pretty fast in this weather on the ice and crust."

But he didn't try to dissuade us. Instead, he advised travelling at night when it would be freezing. The dogs would work better at night as well, he said, when it wasn't so hot.

"You gonna go by the farm and that old stage road?" he asked, though it was hardly expressed as a question.

"The more I look at that open water here, Danny, the less I like the idea of river travel," I admitted. "I think we really would be safer on the old road."

I glanced over at Jan who'd been listening quietly with a far-away look in her eyes. She didn't smile. "The stage road sounds better to me, too," she stated, "if we go on."

There was no emphasis on the 'if' in her voice. It was calmly spoken

– added almost as an afterthought or clarification. But that 'if' was a subtle reminder that Jan had still not committed herself to any one choice. We'd eliminated only one of three options. Jan still had a veto in her hands and we could be headed back out to Pelly Crossing.

The pale pink sunset had been two hours past when our friends left, Danny promising to be our alarm clock next morning. Jan started packing away the gear and fried some bannock to eat for a quick breakfast. The Indians sometimes called bannock *frybread*, I told Jan, and their cakes are deep-fried in lard or other grease. Sort of a cross between a donut and a scone. It is said that whoever can fry a truly cosmic bannock will always find the right path in life.

"The Indians believe that?" Jan asked incredulously. "Abby said that?"

"Okay, I made up that last part," I admitted. "But Danny makes a mean bannock – he puts Tang orange crystals in his – and he's got a pretty amazing life."

I stepped outside to arrange the harnesses and do a last check on the dogs. They were all nestled peacefully, each glancing up sleepily as I crept past and shone the flashlight around. My friend Casey waved his fox-like tail casually as he waited for extra attention. I rubbed his warm bare tummy and then scratched his back. His eyes squinted in sheer rapture and he rippled his back muscles as I wriggled my fingers through that thick, soft under-fur. When I looked up, I could see Tuk waging his tail, obviously pleased at the sight. Rafferty was swishing his shaggy tail, too – and Mitti, and Iskoot. Every dog was waiting, hoping for a goodnight back-rub!

The sky was clear, so I stood a while on the river bank, staring at the stars, and sucking in that cool, clear Yukon air – feeling at home in this raw country. The snow and ice glowed silvery-blue in the moonlight. There was enough starlight and reflection to see quite clearly the rough basalt cliffs across the wide river and to make out the hills and islands downriver towards Dawson City. The Yukon River's great open wound undulated an oily black – it had lengthened considerably even during our short stay. The undercurrent monster would not be resting tonight or any night or day over the next weeks.

We'll meet you again at Stewart River, I thought, and looked away, to appreciate the comforting silhouettes of the abandoned town, the curled dogs and our battered toboggan.

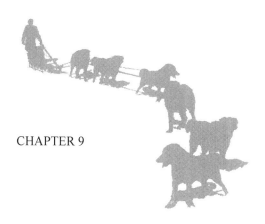

CHAPTER 9

JAN DECIDES

A buzzing – like an insect across the room. A mosquito? A bee… But why is it whining? Now it sounds like a chain saw…

Where am I? What's the matter? Do I have to wake up?

My head was thick, my mind reeling, and my mouth tasted like a sewer. I squinted in the darkness, waiting for a few answers. The whine was progressively louder, more frantic, more insistent. It was clearly a high-revving gas engine approaching quickly. An airplane? I could barely make out the dusky shape of a window and a table beneath it… and a cabin door…

And then I realized where I was – at Fort Selkirk, in the tourist cabin. I jumped up and ran to the door in bare feet to say hello to Danny Roberts. The air outside was crisp. It washed over me like a cold shower, invading my lungs with a chilling freshness. Danny was sitting on the snowmachine, shivering in his parka.

"It's seven o'clock now," he yelled over the engine roar. "Cold, too!" Danny was grinning at my bare toes on the doorsill.

"Yep, I can feel it!" I grinned back. "Thanks for waking us! Have a good trip into town!" We were both shouting and gesturing broadly. A fog of condensing exhaust was swirling around our knees.

"I got something for you!" Danny hollered and tossed me a brown paper bundle. "Moose! Steaks! You can fry them!"

"Hey, great! Awesome! Thanks!" I shouted as he gunned the motor and pulled forward. Then he hesitated.

"When you go," he called back, "don't go too near my cabin or the dogs will get upset! Go way around – I don't want any broken snaps!"

"Okay! We'll do that! See you, Danny!"

He roared off, his red tail-light weaving great Ss through the dark town as he threaded his way around fence posts and abandoned wagons. The roar quickly faded to a whine… then to the buzzing of a summer insect – a strange sound on such a cold, clean morning. By the bite in the air, I knew the temperature was close to zero Fahrenheit. It was certainly no weather to be standing about in bare feet: my toes were now quite numb. As I turned to go back into the cabin, I squinted and could just make out that Rafferty wasn't where I'd tied him. He was, of course, four posts over, curled up beside Flander. A length of chain was still attached to his collar. "If only he would pull the toboggan with half that determination!" I muttered and reached for an armload of wood for the stove.

Jan was up and dressed before I had the fire lit. She started rolling sleeping bags and gathering pots and pans, but looked tired and wasn't saying much. I tried an Eagles cassette in our little tape player, hoping to cheer up the mood, but all the songs were about lonesome, homesick and/or dying cowboys. Jan began making notes in her diary. After three songs I shut it off and we ate our cold bannock in silence.

When Jan slipped out to the outhouse, I shamelessly peeked at the latest diary entry, wanting to understand her mood. Just maybe, my ego was telling me, she was confiding to her paper muse that she really did want to get lucky with me – but was too shy! But no, of course, she wasn't thinking like a guy; her confessions were not about me or sex at all. And, for her, the question of continuing to Dawson involved other factors beyond our personal safety: there was mention of nightmares about unpaid bills and truck payments and her uncertain ambitions in life. "What 2 do?" she'd written. Jan's multiple city-life decisions were competing for attention – no wonder she looked frazzled.

For me, the choice was less complicated. I was also broke but had neither debts nor obligations – nor even vague career ambitions. I'd always found employment, whether as a labourer or surveyor or whatever, whenever the need arose. Life had always unfolded before me in a relatively worry-free fashion. Delaying our return to 'civilized life' simply postponed the need for money (and, shudder, working for someone else). I definitely wanted to give the overland route our best shot now that we were here.

In sharp contrast to Jan's tense mood, the dogs were happy and full of zip after their day's rest – so eager to go that we were able to start for once without a hint of a fight. Jan skied ahead, making a wide detour around Danny's cabin. I followed with our six bright-eyed workers, riding the brake to keep from skidding into the old town's various ruins and debris piles. Back-tracking on Danny's trail out of town, Iskoot wanted to run, so Jan was towed behind us in water-skier fashion. I sang to the dogs – something Abby Roberts had recommended – and called out a warning to Jan each time a dog dropped a deposit on the trail so she could spread her skis to avoid the steaming brown smear. For a novice, she displayed remarkable balance and control at this manoeuvre, though

Our most reliable lead dogs: Casey the Wonder Dog (left) and Iskoot take a break in the sun.

the idea of what she would fall into may have had an inspirational effect on her performance, too.

Down on the river ice, the dogs slowed and Jan was once again the pace setter. Iskoot eagerly followed right behind – a bit too eagerly at times. There was little for me to do except balance the toboggan on corners and slow the dogs from tromping on the tails of Jan's skis. I had to stamp my feet and bang my mitts together to keep warm. The storm had left a burden of snow on the forest. As the sun came out and the morning air warmed, great white clumps cascaded through the branches, startling the dogs from their daydreams as they trotted along methodically. In what seemed like no time at all, we were at the Lammers' place again.

Jan ran up to see John and Mickey while I minded the dogs. All six conveniently lay down in their harnesses and fell asleep in the sun, allowing me to sit on the toboggan with my feet up and the morning sun on my face.

Although there were wool mittens inside my moosehide gauntlets, the morning air was far too cold for inactive fingers. I clenched and unclenched them, trying to stir the circulation. Finally I resorted to a trick every Canadian school kid knows: worrying a tiny fluffball of wool with my fingertips. "This isn't a bad life after all," I said to the crew and closed my eyes.

High on the bank, Jan wasn't relaxing. John Lammers 'heavily advised' her against heading overland toward Dawson City. He was a veteran of many winters in the Yukon wilderness and thought it most unwise to attempt such a journey at this time of year. And if she did go, how would the authorities be notified of trouble? When would people know to begin a search? What preparations had we made for emergencies? Did we have enough food to wait for the break-up of the river ice if we got stranded?

Jan listened to John's questions, and thought about her commitments back in Whitehorse. She wondered about safety, and about what she would do for rent money. Balanced with the cautions of Danny and Abby and advice from John and Mickey, she weighed my arrogance and aspirations, and her own thirst for the Yukon's magic and mystery. One pull seemed to be labelled 'sensible,' the other was 'adventure.' Then slowly, as the tea was sipped, she felt the flame of her own pride and stubbornness flickering inside her. She thanked the Lammers for both the hospitality and their concern, and slowly made her way down the bank.

"Well, let's get going if we're ever going to get there," she muttered as I blinked the sleep out of my eyes.

I roused the dogs and asked quietly, "Get where?"

"We're taking this dog team to Dawson, aren't we?" she said curtly, and stepped into the ski harnesses.

"I guess we are then!" I laughed and off we went.

It was just noon when we reached Pelly Farm again and chained up the dogs at Hugh's cabin. The sun was blazing down and the temperature above freezing already. The farmers were waiting lunch for us, having learned from Danny we weren't taking the river route and would be passing through today. Jan and I hurried inside the farmhouse to help devour a spread of beef tongue, canned tuna, rice, cornbread, apple betty and, of course, gallons of tea. We decided to wait until evening for the snow crust to re-form before heading off, which left us time to help with afternoon chores.

"We've got just the right job for you, Bruce," Dick laughed and led me out to the hallway cupboards. "A real colourful chore."

I spent the afternoon painting doors and shelves while Jan was recruited to wash dishes and bake desserts. The afternoon passed quickly and we were soon sitting down to another magnificent meal of farm food plus Jan's lemon meringue pie. The six at the table managed to pack away enough food for a dozen loggers but ground to a halt before getting to the second pie, a deep-dish apple. We drank coffee as everyone took turns telling stories and jokes. Finally Dick and Hugh brought out their bundle of topographic maps and we went over the mail route in detail once more. Though neither of them had been beyond Black Creek, they were able to supply many route details gleaned from the decades of story-telling around this very table. Since entertainment value rather than navigational precision had been the motive behind most of the travellers' accounts, we knew to take any information with a grain of salt. The detailed maps covered the route as far as the head of Scroggie Creek. "From there it should be an *easy* fifteen mile jaunt to the Stewart River," Dick teased, "so even Bruce won't be able to get lost. Easy as pie. Easy as eating lemon meringue pie."

"You can borrow these maps on two conditions," Hugh said with great melodrama in his voice. "Mail them back to us as soon as you reach Dawson City and… you have to write us a letter telling what it is really like from here to the Stewart. Maybe someday we'll take a trip over the old stage road ourselves. Though likely we'd do it during the summer and ride the tractor."

On that note, everyone headed off to bed. Hugh presented us with a dozen fresh eggs from the 'girls' in the henhouse – a present to bolster our food supplies – and an alarm clock to wake us for our 1 a.m. start.

"If Danny suggested you travel at night, it must be a good idea," he said just before slipping off to his cabin. "Danny has more years of dog mushing under his belt than everyone else around here put together. You shouldn't have too much trouble following the trails in the moonlight…

"And," here he smiled kindly, "you can always turn around and come back this way if you have to. No shame in that."

"Thanks for all your help, Hugh."

"It's nothing really. I just hope we don't see you again until after break-up. Not that you're not welcome – but I hope you and Jan make it through."

CHAPTER 10

FOLLOWING PETER'S TRAIL IN THE DARK

J an rolled over when I tried to wake her, wrapping herself tightly in the blankets and squeezing up against the wall. "I wanna sleep... I wanna sleep..." she murmured. "I wanna sleep..."

When I was reasonably sure she would be getting up, I tried to sneak downstairs, thinking of that deep-dish apple pie waiting on the kitchen counter. Only three steps down the staircase, my intentions were announced to the world by Marjorie's yappy pet terrier, Zipper. He wouldn't quiet down until Jan joined me on the stairs and squatted to pat his shaggy head.

We heated up some left-over coffee and each had a sliver of pie. Even though I was still full from supper, I wanted a taste – knowing it might be a long time before the next apple pie.

Out in the farmyard, the puddles had a solid ice covering and the bare ground felt firm underfoot. The sound of our steps on the snow also told the temperature, making the telltale crunch of a solid frost. Above us, clouds blocked out the stars and any moonlight. Navigating almost by Braille, we crunch-crunched along the fence line until we reached

Hugh's cabin. Our toboggan and harnesses lay in a pool of yellow kerosene lamp light streaming from the cabin windows. Hugh immediately
came outside to help with the harnessing. I released the dogs one at a
time and collected their chains while Jan and Hugh sorted out the tangled
leather and ropes and coaxed each animal into place. With all the chains
tucked away, I clipped on the skis and prepared to set out ahead along
the farm lane. The dogs seemed totally awed by all this commotion in
the darkness. They appeared both confused and excited, but didn't bark
or whine at all. Jan and Hugh had instructions to hold them back until
I was well ahead. With Casey in lead, the team would gallop until they
caught up to me, encouraging the concept of pulling strongly all night.
Or so I hoped.

Hearing only the creaking of my bamboo poles and the rasping of
skis over snow crust, I skated west down the tree-lined lane, invigorated
by the inhalation of crisp night air and feeling somewhat awed at the
pale blue-gray snow drifts and the pitch black silhouettes of poplars and
fence posts. We are really going to do this, I thought happily, going by
dog team to Dawson!

I reached the end of the lane where the trail forked left onto the river
and right onto the old stage road, before the solemn silence was pierced
by far-away howling. Even from this distance I could make out my pet,
Casey, instigating the commotion. He *hated* to be left behind. When the
noise abruptly ended, I knew the chase was on.

The old road, carved from one wall of the creek ravine, climbed
steadily above the farm fields. Peter Isaac's snowmachine track wove
back and forth, from one snow-covered rut to the other, an undulating
corduroy pathway into the hills. I stomped my skis for extra traction to
mount each successive rise. Then, suddenly, I could hear Mitti's staccato

barking. I stopped and listened… Growls and snarls… Jan's shouting… I turned and raced back.

The fight was over but the tempers were still hot back at the junction. Good ol' Casey the Wonder Dog had taken the trail towards Fort Selkirk, and then changed his mind, tangling the team and tipping the toboggan. The dogs seized the opportunity to have a big free-for-all, busting two harnesses and leaving Iskoot with a small red badge of courage on his left ear.

"Delays! Delays! Delays!" Jan shouted at me, the dogs, the sky. "Something is always going wrong!"

Jan swore at the dogs, me, the overturned toboggan and 'this whole stupid idea.' I had a hunch, though, that mostly she wanted to be back in bed sleeping. We had to use a flashlight to find replacement harnessing from a duffle bag on the toboggan – it was still that dark. I glanced at my pocket watch when we finally moved on: two-thirty. Back at his cabin, Hugh had likely heard the commotion and would be wishing us well from his warm bed.

The trail up the ravine seemed much steeper for the dogs and their load than it had been for a single skier. I stayed close to help right the toboggan, which threatened to tip each time the skidoo track switched ruts. A load of almost 300 pounds of freight was no easy matter to right, and yet Jan often managed by herself. This barmaid was certainly determined and she was getting stronger by the day. She walked behind the toboggan and pushed up some of the hills, while I scampered ahead of Casey, urging the dogs to lean into their task. For now, the skis stayed lashed on top of the load.

After two miles, Jan ran ahead for a spell. Her eyes were better in the darkness than mine. I needed the flashlight to see the trail and somehow she managed without. At one point, I heard a metallic clunk at my feet and stopped the dogs. With the flashlight's help, I looked about on the tail of the toboggan and walked back along the trail, searching for whatever had dropped from the kit bag tied to the handlebars. Nothing. A subsequent check through the bag revealed that the pliers were missing! How would we fix dog chains and toboggan bolts without pliers?

For twenty minutes we kicked through the loose snow and thoroughly scoured the area, but to no avail. The pliers seemed to have simply vanished. We gave up and pushed on, cursing our bad luck and both muttering about "what could go wrong next?" Now I, too, was wishing to be back in a warm bed.

The sky brightened a touch just after four and we stopped for a snack at the spot where Peter's snowmachine trail veered away from the stage road right-of-way. This, I explained as we drank hot grapefruit juice from the thermos and ate old, cold bannock from yesterday's breakfast, was the route down Horsefell Creek to Peter Isaac's Black Creek camp. Following Peter's trail would be somewhat longer than going straight along the old mail route, I explained, but having a packed surface should more than compensate. Jan's look of dismay caught me by surprise. I was about to elaborate on my reasoning when she cut me off.

"—My knife. I can't find it. It's gone too!"

"You've checked all your pockets? How about in the kitchen box?"

"I just looked. I know I had it in my pocket when we started this morning. Now it's not there!"

She looked quite miserable, her head drooped forward and brow wrinkled. Her shoulders were slumped and she kicked at the snow in frustration. The knife was a cheap imitation Swiss Army-style jackknife that I'd lent her for the trip, but it was one of only three knives we'd brought.

"Don't worry," I said, trying to cheer her up. "We're almost out of canned food anyway. And even if we lost all the knives, Tuk would open cans for us if we could convince him there was food inside."

Big white Tuk wagged his tail at the mention of his name and Jan went over and rubbed his tummy. Then she made the rounds to scratch every chin and behind every ear. By the time she'd run out of dogs, she was almost smiling again.

Peter's trail was narrow, winding through willows, birch stands, climbing now onto a ridge, then keeping to a creek bed, mostly descending in altitude. We travelled easily, the dogs behaving better. Perhaps it was my voice, but more likely it was the downhill trail. Jan ran ahead in her moccasins and would call: "Come on, Iskoot! Here, puppies! Come on, doggies!" to encourage them.

Sometimes the path was so narrow through the dense spruce that Peter's skidoo sled had scarred the bark on both sides. In such close quarters, the dogs' trot felt alarmingly fast. I ducked under low branches and held on tight, pedalling to steer the toboggan around trunks and between muskeg hummocks. Out in the more open forest, I could relax and appreciate the majestic stillness, noting the birch and snow wore the same soft pastels as the rising sun.

Miles of very straight, slightly-downhill stretches were easily eaten up by the dogs' steady gait. Now the trail abruptly angled west, hugging the north slope of a creek ravine. At one point we reached a fork but the right hand choice didn't appear as well travelled, so we continued on the left. We both hugged the toboggan during a wild, furious gallop that brought us down through a narrow canyon and suddenly out into a

clearing. Two dilapidated log buildings squatted on a bank, tilted relics looking out across a mile of river ice. This was the Yukon River, of
course, snow-covered and quiet here, with no sign anywhere of open
water.

I pulled out the Bradleys' maps while Jan explored the cabins. She
held up an empty flour bag and a current *Field & Stream* magazine from
the doorway to illustrate recent occupancy. Peter must have used these
buildings as well as a Black Creek camp when trapping this section. This
was Horsefell Creek, I reckoned – we'd chosen the wrong fork at that last
junction. The extra distance travelled would measure almost three miles
by the time we retraced our tracks to the fork.

"Look at this mouse," Jan called out from the far side of the larger
cabin. "He's all white!"

As she focused her camera on the white nose poking from a burrow
in the sod roof, the mouse's neck stretched and stretched and stretched.
Eventually it became clear that this wasn't a white mouse at all, it was a
weasel! The little fellow finally came all the way out, turned to show us
his long black-tipped tail, and then skittered back deep into the sod. I explained that weasels are trapped during winter for their fur and the resulting coats are called 'ermine', which has a better ring to it than 'weasel
coat'. Soon this white fellow would revert to his summer brown colour.

I glanced at my watch and was surprised to read 8 a.m. already. Jan
too had thought it was much earlier, although she had an explanation – it
was the flying saucers' doing. She'd noticed the strange blue lights again
and now asked if I was happy that extra-terrestrials were interested in us.

They'll be making quite a collection of pliers, knives and lost mitts
if they follow us right to Dawson, was my only thought.

With a half-hour's rest after the wild rush down, the dogs needed

Jan tends a smokey fire. She is melting snow for the dogs' supper.
Eating so quickly, they won't care about a few needles and twigs.

little encouragement to head out again. Jan ran ahead and I jogged behind as they hustled through the canyon and back up the ravine to the
forks. The proper track kept to high ground, following an upper bench
through mixed forest. After a mile, the forest thinned to give us an un-
impeded view of the Yukon valley. We were travelling on a flat plateau,
along the edge of a steep 200-foot-high cliff dropping straight down to
the river. This was a continuation of the volcanic basalt walls we'd seen
opposite Fort Selkirk at the mouth of the Pelly. From here the river ice
looked solid and flat but I knew that the crinkles on that snowy mantle
were massive ice jams and crevasses. So far the trail had been enjoyable.
I certainly didn't miss the anxiety of ice travel at all.

By noon we'd left the forest behind and were moving through

meadow-like fields. We were both walking zombies, hardly talking but happy to have covered so much distance. We'd reached the Black Creek watershed and were glad to call camp under a huge lone spruce. Some trees were born to sleep under; this one formed a magnificent roof sheltering enough bare, dry ground for many people.

Jan proposed that the dogs be allowed to run free for a few minutes and I was too tired to argue. Having a team of half-pets ensures that at least one dog will be sucky enough to be a nuisance, but we hardly expected all six trying to sleep on us as we laid out on our sleeping bags under the warm afternoon sun. And needy dogs seem to be jealous dogs – within minutes minor skirmishes erupted involving just about every combination and permutation of the team. Flander soon sported a few bleeding cuts to put him in the purple heart medal club that Tuk and Rafferty usually presided over.

Between rounds of the fracas, Jan wrote a diary entry that there were 'minor dissensions amongst the troops.' Rafferty cowered at the foot of Jan's sleeping bag for protection against Tuk, who was intent on fighting even though he always lost. Jan finally agreed that it was a mistake to let them loose when Rafferty began to climb *into* the bag with her.

Most of the dogs had been chained, and the two loose ones relatively quiet, when I began to rustle up our supper. All day long I'd been looking forward to feasting on the moose meat Danny Roberts had given us. The steaks would go a long way towards restoring the energy – mental and physical – expended over the day's 12-hour, 20-plus-mile trek. I was unpacking the food box, laying out onions and spices beside me, planning a gourmet production when Tuk dashed over and grabbed the two moose steaks! He bounded off into the woods. I followed, screaming and cursing and leaping through the deep snow. He circled a large poplar.

I cut him off. He swerved just out of reach. I took a chance and dived over a low bush. One hand gripped a hind leg and he fell with a thud. I scrambled forward on hands and knees, wrestling to get to the front end of this squirming canine... I found only a bloody wrapper hanging from his jaws.

Tuk's tail was beating a loud, taunting rhythm on the snow and an unmistakeable smirk had formed on his ugly face. Those big brown eyes were just too smug for me to bear. I blew up. Furious, I pounded on his side until my arm was sore. When I'd vented my anger and stood up trembling and weak, Tuk simply wagged his tail happily! He gazed gleefully at the food box, anxious for a repeat performance. He was immediately chained up. And, though he was not fed when the others were served their evening crunchies, Tuk never made a murmur of a fuss about being passed by.

It was that night that I started the *Eat List*. This was a mental record, updated continuously, of which dog we would kill and eat first, if we ran out of food. Eating dog flesh was hardly appealing but tonight there was one dog I'd rather see dead than alive.

It was dark by the time our vegetarian meal was over and we were snuggled down in our bags. Above us, through the sweeping branches, stars twinkled and a slice of moon slipped from behind a wisp of cloud. Overhead, a great owl was hooting, his call sometimes very near, sometimes high up, as he patrolled the meadows hunting for his meat.

CHAPTER 11

CROSSING THE MUSKEG

Monday mornings can have a depressing quality – even 1,500 miles north of the nearest bustling metropolis. Jan and I dragged ourselves from the warmth of our down bags and squatted, shivering, around a small breakfast fire. The snow we melted for tea water produced disgusting bonuses: spruce needles, twigs, rabbit droppings and a dead mouse. Packing up seemed to take forever. Though nothing was really wrong, something just didn't feel 100% right either. Blame it on the day of the week perhaps.

When we finally got the dog team rolling, it was apparent that this day was sure to get hot and sloppy. The ice crust wouldn't last more than a few hours. I was skiing, following a plan to ski first when the dogs were fresh and able to follow my pace, and then let Jan ski later in the day at her slower speed. I should be able to coax the dogs when they were losing interest and needed a firm hand. That was the plan, for what it was worth. This morning our workers pulled fine and we raced along, stopping for a brief peek inside a crude log building that might have been used as a trapline cabin long ago.

After another mile, we noticed a few chainsaw-marked stumps near the trail and knew we were approaching a modern-day abode. It turned out to be an A-frame log shelter made of logs and poles leaned together along a ridge pole. It was a 12-foot-long peaked roof plunked directly on the ground with no walls. Surrounding this minimalist structure were snowmobile parts, oil cans, scraps of canvas, worn-out cooking pots, saw blades – and there was hint of much more beneath the snow. A penciled declaration on the plank door declared the rough shelter to be used by Peter Isaac and two Silverfox brothers. Inside there wasn't room to stand, and hardly any light, but the small sheet metal stove would have made this an oven-like retreat on 40-below nights.

From this spot there were two trails: one heading almost northeast and the other northwest. I skied a hundred yards along the northeast path before opting for the other trail. Both routes had roughly the same degree of travel, but the left fork was better cleared. Already the sun was softening the crust and making the dogs cranky. Where dense clumps of white spruces sheltered the trail from much snowfall, we came across the occasional bare patch of ground. Here the damp earth grabbed at the toboggan base, arresting the toboggan's momentum and upsetting the dogs' rhythm. They would immediately stop, hoping this was a resting spot – or better yet, where we'd camp.

"No such luck, fellas," Jan would holler. "Get up and get GOING!"

Seeing all this bare ground, my thoughts drifted ahead past Black Creek and Jane, Walhalla and Scroggie creeks to the river ice we'd be facing on the Stewart River. Yet, as if to reassure me, we crossed innumerable ponds and creeks all frozen right through to bottom.

We soon passed out of the mixed forest and into open muskeg, huge tracts of swamp broken only by random stands of scrawny black spruce and thickets of willow bush. Peter's meandering track criss-crossed the broad valley, looping off to a clump of willows where a lynx trap had been set, winding through the giant tussocks of muskeg, skirting some ponds and crossing others. Here a wolf snare had been hung and beyond it the dogs stopped to scratch through the snow for traces of bait from a marten cubby set. As the temperature rose, the dogs could no longer haul the load and the musher as well. Jan walked behind, her boots frequently punching through the trail's thin crust. Peter's skidoo was actually an inch narrower than our toboggan, but repeated trips had packed a slightly wider trail, typically leaving us barely a half-inch of clearance. Either side of the packed surface was calf-deep powdery snow. I took a turn behind and had a new appreciation of how hard Jan had been working. The toboggan would tip or jam into the banks at the slightest provocation. The only way to free it was to stomp around the toboggan through the deep, loose snow and muscle the front back onto the exact centre of the track. Then it was a matter of pushing mightily from behind the toboggan, trying to time the heave with the half-hearted jerk of the dogs responding to: "Okay, GET UP now!!!"

Black Creek had, by this point, split into a dozen pup creeks that snaked across the muskeg, merging and subdividing and generally getting in our way. During one creek crossing, the toboggan slid off Peter's makeshift bridge of three fallen trees and it took both Jan and me and all the dogs straining our utmost to bull it up the steep bank. By now we were thoroughly wet up to the knees from stomping through deep snow and none too happy about the work involved to go such short distances. When the trail veered right and didn't go up the first tributary valley, we were only a bit disappointed. Checking the map, I figured we must be about two miles from the next pup creek's departure from the muskeg, the point at which we should find the old stage road.

Another hour of twisting, tilting trail later, we appeared to be by-passing this next valley as well. Had I choosen the wrong trail out from Peter's A-frame shelter?

The frustration of mushing dogs in poor conditions is a real test of any relationship. Jan and I had kept so much emotion out-front, on-top. If we were angry, we said so – and often neither politely nor tactfully. The underlying worry about our safety was eating away at our nerves. I really surprised myself with sudden outbursts of bad temper, since usually I suppressed, even denied, any anger, and certainly never erupted in curses and ground-stomping as I did now. Today we seemed trapped in a bizarre dog-triggered primal therapy session that might never end. I would have felt worse if Jan hadn't answered in kind, never backing down. Then, almost as quickly as tempers flared, the emotions would dissipate and we'd be laughing foolishly.

"Jeez, did I really just say *that*?" Jan would proclaim with a huge grin. "That was *so* rude!"

"You know, maybe we can stop ourselves from being so angry," I suggested. "It's really not helping anything. Feels good at the moment maybe, but…"

"Yeah, it takes too much energy," Jan agreed. "I'm game to try. Let's save it for when we *really* lose it."

As the hours crept by, the sun's warmth increased steadily. We shed layer after layer of clothing while pushing the dogs and toboggan along the ever-softening track. The crust and packed snow beneath it had deteriorated into a terrible state, like a thin sheet of styrofoam resting on six inches of stale porridge. Every third or fourth step you would break through. Each move increased the anxiety level, whether the crust yielded or held. When the dogs became tangled and the toboggan tipped for the fourth time in a hundred feet, I lashed out with "Well, what did I do wrong this time?" and we were at it again. I ended the conversation with a curt announcement that I would ski ahead alone to scout the route and abruptly poled away.

"Well, how long are you going to be?" Jan called out sheepishly.

For a moment I pretended not to have heard. I almost skied on but I felt suddenly ashamed to be acting so rudely, being mean with the one person who would have to rescue me if I didn't come back. Jan was the only person who had believed in this adventure, who had believed in me and who had worked so hard to get us this far. This was my partner, constantly proving she was capable of just about any performance demanded of her and surprising me with more. I paused for a moment to calm my voice before replying.

"Give me 90 minutes, okay?" Then I added quietly, "I'll be careful. Don't worry." I knew that she would worry though – and felt more secure because of it.

Even with the uncertain crust and despite the worn-out, bare-based skis, I simply oozed up the positive energy that cross-country skiing can give. I love the rhythm of the stride, the exertion, the speed, the beauty and quiet. My emotional batteries were being quick-charged during these oh-so-wonderful moments away from the dogs and toboggan. Sweat beads trickled down my face, tickling the skin under my beard. Salty droplets found their way into the corners of my smile. This I could take more of, I thought.

But after only a quarter mile, the skidoo trail turned abruptly left and was joined from the south by a long, cleared (but unpacked) right-of-way.

Peter's trail was back on the old overland route again – we'd taken the correct fork at his cabin after all.

I skied back. The elapsed time had been only about ten minutes and Jan looked alarmed. "What's wrong?" she asked.

"Not a thing. Not a thing," I laughed and gave her a hug. "Everything is right in the world. The Dawson Road is only a few hundred yards away. I was just on it."

She rolled her eyes and smiled. "It's about time. I was beginning to think someone had moved it during the night."

The sun's rays were beating down relentlessly, almost blinding us with the reflected brightness off the snow. At our feet, six very hot huskies lay panting in their thick fur coats. Wet, pink tongues hung from their jaws, and deep panting sighs signalled their intentions. Before they became any sleepier, we straightened the harnesses and pushed forward along the last lap of our Black Creek detour.

Out on the road, Peter's trail was less firmly packed and much narrower. No doubt the road's straightness had permitted much faster machine travel, plus the openness would have allowed more snow drifting across the track. Despite the trail conditions, the dogs picked up enthusiasm and pulled more spiritedly, dragging the toboggan strongly as it bulldozed a neat half-inch off both sides. For over a mile we trampled onwards, the dogs straining for traction on the thin crust, the toboggan crunching into the banks, grinding over ice crystals and occasionally upsetting. With all their feet, the loaded toboggan, a pair of skis and sometimes the musher's bootprints too, we were packing an excellent trail behind us. Glancing over my shoulder at this legacy, I was reminded of Hugh Bradley's parting comments. Yes, returning to Pelly Farm would be easier, but I sure didn't want to have to finish our trip there.

"A bit of night travelling on this road should be a lot easier than straining through this heat," I called out.

"If that means you want to stop, I'm all for it," said Jan and we halted at the first stand of trees. We'd been travelling almost 12 hours.

We left the dogs in their harnesses, chaining up only the lead dog so they couldn't get too tangled. They were all so tired and over-heated that they were asleep in no time.

Spreading out the tarp over a small area I'd tramped down, we had a dry place to relax, stretch sore muscles, heat some water and have a bird bath. While wet socks and boot liners steamed in front of the fire, we slopped hot, soapy water over sooty faces and sponged out sweaty armpits. Glancing over at the team, I was amused to see that Mitti was following our lead – she was grooming herself thoroughly with feline wipes of her long, thin tongue.

Checking through our supplies after a quick supper, we found two loaf cans of bread were left. I put one in the dog chain bag with cheese and dried meat for tonight's meal stop, while Jan packed away all the other food and cooking gear into the grub box on the toboggan. We planned to try our second starlight run tonight, after sleeping for the rest of the afternoon and evening.

Jan immediately fell asleep in the late afternoon sunshine, but I chose to read for a while to relax first. The book was Frederick Forsyth's *Day of the Jackal*, the spy novel set in France, and I was suddenly struck by the irony of this book choice: in Paris the year before, I had read R.M. Patterson's *Dangerous River*, a true account of life in the Canadian wilderness.

How large and small is this world, I thought, and how interconnected. What would be the complete opposite, the counterpart to our snail's pace crawl through the hills, searching for answers in traditions almost forgotten?

Before turning in, I filled the thermos with hot coffee and moved the steaming socks back a bit from the heat. As I lay in my bag, feeling noticeably cleaner for having had that bird bath, I happened to notice a thread-like white line being drawn silently across the deep blue sky. Seven miles above us, a US Strategic Air Command bomber was patrolling, posed to participate in a nuclear war that could end all life on this planet. That answered my question.

CHAPTER 12

NIGHT MOVES

Something woke me at midnight – perhaps an owl calling, perhaps stomach rumblings from drinking too much coffee. Groggily we put on our many layers of clothing and stuffed the sleeping bags into their sack. Jamming all that down insulation into a small container must rate as one of the coldest chores imaginable. The frosted nylon coverings were too slippery to grip with mitts on. Bare hands had to be used and that meant freezing our fingertips. With arms crossed and numb hands painfully thawing under my armpits, I tried to imagine a warm-up fire energizing me, toasting my face and steaming my clothes. But this was not morning, and there would be no campfire.

The dogs were still in harness except Iskoot who had gnawed his way to freedom. He lay nestled only four feet away, sharing an icy shelf with Casey. The fur on their faces and necks was crusted with crystals of frozen breath. Looking surprised, even alarmed, that we wanted them to wake up, one by one the team slowly rose to their feet, stretched, shook thoroughly and yawned. "Don't you know it's night-time?" their puzzled looks asked. "Can't you see that it's dark?" But we set out anyway.

Our flashlight gradually weakened until its beam was of little use. Jan and I took turns skiing ahead, she managing quite well, while I stumbled on each unseen ridge or depression. For this night travel I'd opted to wear glasses instead of my contact lenses. Squinting through my thick spectacles into the gloom, my eyes registered bear-shapes and wolverines instead of bushes, and smiling crocodiles for each fallen tree. Fortunately, there was little chance of losing the packed trail – the instant a ski tip veered into the deeper snow, my forward momentum was halted.

The crew displayed their reluctance in a variety of ways. Our two biggest dogs, Tuk and Rafferty, appeared to be asleep on their feet. Little Iskoot had to be picked up and stood on his feet each time we paused. He was clearly still fatigued from struggling yesterday in the wet snow, so we finally removed his harness and let the white pup run along behind. Within minutes, though, he was energetically running up beside the others, playfully nipping Casey's orange ears and cross-checking him into the deep snow. As a compromise, I harnessed Iskoot immediately behind his playmate and hoped he wouldn't over-exhaust himself. Mitti demanded frequent stops to lick her feet and chew at the snowballs sticking to the hairs between her pads. Flander discovered he could climb halfway out of his harness by jerking back suddenly to slip the neck strap over his head. He and I had quite a struggle of wills before he eventually decided that half-freedom wasn't worth my wrath. And, as usual, each mutt waited for a particularly strategic moment – always an uphill – to have his or her own private poo stop.

Although the snow was colder now, it was also deeper. There was virtually no crust, so the front dogs were high-stepping to trample a trail for the others. On the straight stretches, the toboggan slid easily on top of the granular snow but curved sections were a different matter. There the curl either caught on the inside bank or overshot to the outside. Approaching each turn, I had to lean on the handlebars to tilt the toboggan's base, then pump with one foot to help the toboggan swivel around the bend. On steep uphills, I'd hop right off and push, then run to catch up on the downhill. Through level areas, without the musher's weight on the sled, the dogs trotted slightly faster than a human's walking pace. Carrying the musher meant only half that speed. I'd trudge behind for a minute, my big pac boots sinking into the trail as if it were loose beach sand – then I'd jog a bit, trying to be close at hand whenever a curve loomed out of the dark.

After three hours (perhaps six miles) of long gradual uphills, and as the first glow of dawn began to light the sky, we came to a clearing: a broad snowy basin ringed by massive ghostly-grey hills. The dark whiskers near the base of each mount were the last trees to survive at this altitude. We would be leaving tree-line as we ascended further. Here, overlooking the basin, and on the bank of the highest spring to feed Black Creek were the remains of Black Creek Roadhouse. These road-houses had been built for the White Pass & Yukon Route Company who had constructed this road and held the early mail contracts from railhead at Whitehorse through to Dawson City. Hugh had told us to expect a structure about every twenty miles, a customary distance for changing or resting horses.

"If only we were here seventy years ago," Jan said wistfully. "There'd be warm meals and beds and someone to look after the dogs. It would have been one hell of a lot easier then."

The roadhouse was in ruins. It had been a two-storey monster but now the pole roof lay on the floor in a jumbled pile, rotting under a wet snow load it could no longer bear. Behind it was a small cabin that had been used by Peter Isaac as a stop-over shack. It had a sturdy pole roof that looked newer than the rest of the construction. The truth of a Northern adage that 'a cabin lasts only as long as its roof' was evident here: the roadhouse walls were rotting and tumbling down, while this cabin was still sturdy. The cabin's plank door wasn't locked, just propped shut with a stick. Inside there was a small sheet metal stove and a crude bunk against one wall. In the failing beam of the flashlight, I saw empty flour bags, empty tins and the inevitable outdoor magazines. If they had voices, the snowmobile parts heaped in one corner could probably tell of breakdowns at 50° below. The life of a trapper was certainly no luxury.

Outside again, I spotted Jan standing behind the toboggan, digging through the dog chain bag with a worried look on her face. She glanced up, saw me watching and her face fell.

"The bread's gone," she said. "It must have fallen out one of those times we tipped... I'm so sorry..."

"And the dried meat?" I asked, trying to remain calm.

"Not here either," she said timidly.

"S-H-I-T!" I screamed and closed my eyes. A wave of heat rose from my chest and engulfed my face. I wanted to grab something and break it. The jerked beef and rye loaf were supposed to be our next two days' lunch as well.

"I'm sorry..." Her voice was small and timid.

I turned and walked away, over to the garbage pile that was once a roadhouse. There I stared out over the glaciered spring and breathed deeply, venting foggy streams into the dusky air. At last, I pulled a long scrap of canvas from the debris and sat on it in the snowbank. Jan slumped down beside me and leaned back wearily against the snow.

"It's not your fault," I whispered. "I packed that bag."

Her eyes were closed and she remained silent.

"It's this bloody travelling in the dark. We can't afford to lose anything more... From now on, let's travel only by day... Okay?"

This time her head nodded slightly. I wriggled down further in my seat and pulled my parka tight around me. We were tired, hungry and frustrated. In a few moments we were also asleep.

Sunrise had tip-toed past and the sky was clear when I next opened my eyes. About ninety minutes had elapsed. The dogs, still in their traces, were nestled and dozing peacefully. I glanced beside me: Jan was still sleeping in her snow chair, but her body warmth was slowly melting the snow and wetting her parka.

Time to push on, I thought, sighing deeply, before the trail gets too warm. We can sleep when it's hot later.

I put one hand on her knee and said softly, "Come on, Jan, let's go now."

She opened her eyes, stared blankly for a moment and then shook herself.

"Yep," she muttered and struggled to her feet.

Some holiday this is turning out to be for her, I was thinking as Jan walked around stiffly, patting dog heads while visibly shaking off the mantle of sleep. How long can she keep up? How long can I keep this pace, for that matter?

"Who skis?" she asked simply and I volunteered. A wide-awake Mitti barked a gruff reveille and the other five little soldiers struggled to their feet, stretched, shook, yawned and sniffed the air. They were perhaps too groggy to argue with any orders this early.

I kicked off and poled myself past the team, around the rubble of

Black Creek Roadhouse and down a slope across the glaciered spring. I
waited out on the wide ice surface – it was easily a hundred feet across
– until Jan cleared the roadhouse bend in pursuit. It was not so long ago
that this tributary of Black Creek would have had its own name and the
innkeeper's children playing on its banks, a horse to help draw water
from a hole chopped through the clear, thick ice, water for the roadhouse
staff and the travellers on the overland stage...

"Clear the track!" Jan yelled, so I hurried on, skittering across the
glassy surface and on up the far bank. The dogs galloped eagerly behind.

Soon, however, the road began to climb steadily and our pace slowed
to the typical crawl. After a half-hour, I traded roles and was quickly
bathed in sweat from pushing up the steep inclines and coaching the
dogs. In contrast, Jan had her first real opportunity this morning to get
ahead and away from us and merrily took photographs of the high tundra's windswept snow formations and of the increasingly spectacular
alpine vista. The forest near the road was dwindling away, the diameters
of the remaining stunted trees decreasing as we approached tree-line.
Although we continued climbing up to the pass, the grade was gradual
and the dogs were able to keep up to Ms. Prenty. Just over the saddle
before us, 4,000-foot mountains thrust skyward, shouting for attention
as we marched onward. Far ahead, golden in the morning sun, one spire
towered above the rest. This was our first view of Pyroxene Mountain. I
pulled out the map and pointed out its position to Jan while she unpacked
the makings for a cold brunch.

"After a few more miles of this tundra, we'll have a completely
new watershed," I said. "Soon we'll be drinking water that flows not
into the Pelly or Yukon as before, but into the Stewart River. We'll cross
Jane Creek, climb another pass into the Walhalla Creek valley, and then

follow that until it merges with Alberta Creek and then Scroggie Creek."
I had to pause for breath – even saying all this was tiring. "Then, maybe
20 miles of packing trail past where Peter's track ends and we'll be at the
Stewart River."

"And from there, how far?" Jan asked without much enthusiasm.

"About 100 miles if we go down the Stewart to the Yukon River and
follow the packed trail into Dawson. That part should be easy – like a
sidewalk, almost a highway from all the traffic of snowmobiles and dog
teams."

"Yeah, a piece of cake. Nothing to it," Jan muttered stoically. "Sure.
We'll just keep Pyroxene Mountain on our left. Nothing to it. A holiday
from here on…"

She was muttering something about taking her next f***ing holiday
in Hawaii as we moved out. The high winds common at this altitude had
hard-packed the trail, creating ideal conditions for the dogs. This morning, with a cool tail wind, we dashed across the tundra – Jan had to brake
occasionally to allow me to stay ahead. Floppy-eared little Iskoot in lead
position was full of energy and the others responded enthusiastically. I
stretched my strides and raced until my head was dizzy. As long as the
dogs had the urge, I certainly wanted to make time.

"Yahooooo!" Jan sang as she held tight to the handlebars.

How could Hawaii be this wonderful? I giggled to myself and sprinted on.

I almost swept past without noticing two sets of footprints crossing
the road. The dog's sniffing noses soon pointed out two circular packed
depressions at roadside, the bed last night for a mother caribou and her
calf. If the dogs were anxious before, now they had to be termed frantic.
Iskoot kept trying to bolt past me as all ran with heads high and eyes

scanning the horizon for big game. Despite the vigilance, however, the sudden explosion into flight of a snow-white ptarmigan sitting perfectly camouflaged on the trail startled us all.

Down a gentle descent we went, watching as stubby bushes gathered in sheltered folds, increasing in density and scale as we dropped in altitude. Each snowy basin around us was, we knew, contributing from under its white covering a trickle of melt water to form Jane Creek. Then, the terrain abruptly folded and high hills rose to enclose our trail. The road swept grandly left and we were suddenly here: Jane Creek's crossing. It was noon and we halted to grab our breath.

For a few minutes, Jan and I sat on the toboggan to discuss strategy. From our midnight start, we'd travelled over ten hours already today and covered about fifteen miles, the last part blissfully easy, but much before that a sustained grunt. We felt relieved, though, to have made good progress, and more than a little proud of ourselves. But what to do from here? There was no shelter, and little material for firewood, so we pretty well had to carry on.

Ahead of us we could see the thin line of our route snaking up a gray slope. I checked the topo map and reported that we were now 1,900 feet above sea level. In passing over the hill before us – crossing over to the Walhalla Creek valley – we would have to attain 2,700 feet. The difference was only 800 feet, I explained, "sort of like climbing an 80-storey building."

"I don't think we'll make it," said Jan.

"Sure we can."

"The dogs are pretty tired."

"We'll certainly sleep better on the far side."

"It's pretty hot. The toboggan isn't sliding too well – it's starting to grab."

"Let's give it a try."

We gave it a try. A damn good try. We pushed and cursed and tried again, straining and sweating like Turks in a steam bath under that mid-day sun. We coaxed and pleaded with the dogs, threatened to feed them to the circling ravens, then massaged their little shoulders after every fifty feet gained. Finally, we sat on the hillside in our T-shirts and ate snow and looked back across the valley. Far, far below and behind us we could see the Jane Creek crossing. We hadn't made it. We were com-pletely spent about three-quarters of the way up to the pass. Around us was the gray and black stubble of a charred forest, the sobering legacy of a forest fire many decades past. These bleak skeletons would have to cook our meals, warm our bodies and somehow shelter us from the dark storm clouds now gathering over Black Creek.

"Doesn't look good," I said, nodding toward the ominous weather front.

"Let's get fed before it hits," Jan said matter-of-factly.

"Yep. Okay. We can think about spending tomorrow night at Peter's cabin at Scroggie Creek."

By now the pattern of setting camp had become routine. Hardly a word was spoken as we moved from task to task. Both knew what needed doing.

Off the narrow snowmobile track, the loose snow was thigh-deep. I ploughed through, making six paths to six burnt trees to chain up six dogs. I think they were all asleep before I had an armload of wood gath-ered. They had pulled almost thirteen hours; they had a right to be tired. But then, so did we.

While Jan built a bonfire to cook our food and a hot meal for the crew, I dug a sleeping pit with a snowshoe. Then I chopped some long poles to support our tarp and was just installing it when the first flakes began to drift down. The accompanying chill felt like someone had left a freezer door open. I shivered and pulled up my parka hood. Soon the snow was swirling around us as the storm's tempo picked up. When the wind changed direction, I moved the poles, tightened ropes, re-aligned our sleeping bags, propped up the lee side, then sat a moment to catch my breath before the direction shifted again.

Jan had already spilled most of one meal when the fire melted down through the packed snow, tilted abruptly, and dumped the grill and pots into the ashes. She sighed deeply and reached over into the food box to begin again.

"Am I ever S-T-U-P-I-D," she muttered.

Leaning against my pack under the tarp, with my eyes half closed and barely enough energy to speak, I was thinking instead of her incredible stamina. "Who'd ever believe this back at the Edgewater Tavern?" I whispered.

Jan rocked slowly back and forth, staring into the flames.

"Boy, I could use a beer right now," she said finally, letting out a long sigh.

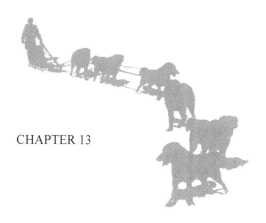

CHAPTER 13

TO HEAVEN AND BACK

Granddad once told me about winter nights in the trenches during World War One. The infantry men were issued two woollen blankets each. They wrapped these around their greatcoats and tried to find a relatively dry sleeping spot out of the rain, the icy water and mud.

"Did you manage to be warm enough, Granddad? How did you make it through the winter like that?" I had asked him.

"We shivered a lot," he answered after a moment's reflection. "All the time we shivered, or we wouldn't have stayed alive."

Then, with a half-smile, he added, "You can stay pretty warm just shivering like that, kiddo."

He enlisted a few months before his 16th birthday – having lied about his age – and survived three winters at the front. He was gassed and hospitalized from shrapnel wounds. Yet I never heard him complain or be bitter about those incredible hardships.

Here on the unnamed pass between Jane and Walhalla creeks, daylight had arrived and I was cold and shivering. But I thought about Granddad and how the situation could be much worse – at least no one

The old stage road will take us over high alpine passes, above the tree line. We are headed for Walhalla, the Heavenly Hall of the Slain.

was shooting at us – and let myself shiver violently while rubbing my hands roughly over my neck and upper arms to stimulate circulation. A quarter-inch of frost had formed overnight around the opening of the sleeping bag. Seen from inside, the morning light was silhouetting the clumps of damp goose down. I wondered if Granddad's two blankets might have been warmer.

A few minutes later, I had a fire going in the big melt hole where Jan had prepared last night's suppers. When there was water boiling, I woke her and handed her a cup of instant coffee. She told me she'd been cold much of the night but didn't feel too bad except for her feet. She held them by the flames and cried, "Ouch, ouch!" as they thawed.

It would be *almost easy* from here on, I explained. From the summit just above us it would be essentially downhill all the way to Dawson City. If we could make it today to the junction with Scroggie Creek, then two more days would see us at Stewart Island and onto the snowmobile trails right to Dawson. Jan just nodded, probably not believing a word I was saying about the optimistic schedule.

When we rolled and stuffed the sleeping bags, I noticed they were quite wet on the underside. There had been no spruce boughs to place underneath. Even the closed-cell foam pads were wet enough to have frozen to the snow below us – we had to be very careful prying them up so as not to rip them. Peter had said there was a good cabin at Scroggie where his trail ended. We'd need that shelter to dry our bedding.

By 9:30 we were underway once again, Jan ahead on the skis and the dogs pulling strongly. We had managed another start without a dog fight and the extra energy was noticeable and appreciated. Although it was a steep grade with another inch of fresh snow over the too-narrow skidoo track, I was able to ride the toboggan most of the way up and didn't even have to push. Iskoot was leading again with Casey just behind, then Flander, Rafferty and Mitti. Tuk was wheel dog. He seemed to like that position where he didn't have to pay much attention to anything but Mitti's butt.

On the summit we broke into overwhelming sunshine and renewed optimism. Walhalla is a Norse name for the Heavenly Hall of the Slain, and this version was otherworldly bright. Dazzling snowflake diamonds blanketed the ground. Each exhale became a cotton-fluff cloud, clinging as frost to the soft fur of the dogs and around the hood of my parka. Jan's hood was thrown back and heat waves shimmered above her head. She too had silvery tips on her hair. God, she's surely an angel, I thought.

The only milepost we found. That's Iskoot in lead, then Casey, Flander and Rafferty. Behind them would be Mitti and Tuk.

Casey bit into the snowbank, bit again, munching on the cooling crystals as he trotted. Rafferty was smiling and waving his tall black plume-like tail from side to side with each stride. Mitti, straining to look past him, around him or over him, barked quickly each time she caught sight of Jan ahead. Then she lowered her head and pulled harder. "Let's catch up. Let's go," Mitti barked.

And go we did. Some moments are magical. The heart is light, the world is right and white – and bright. Downwards we flew, Janet skiing like a dancer through time, the dogs galloping rhythmically, their paws throwing up a scatter of new snow onto the wooden curl of the toboggan. On the tail I leaned back in the lightness and laughed. "Mush! Yippeeeee!"

Pyroxene Mountain was only seven miles away, then five... We started uphill to reach a high bench. The trees were larger, the forest denser here on this south-facing slope. The road cruised through; the ground had been scarcely disturbed during road construction, only trees removed and the forest floor levelled for the mail stage sleighs. It was easy to imagine this road as it was back in the day, well packed and dotted with horse manure. Now and then we would spot an axe-marked stump or a plank leaning against a tree but little else historical – until I spotted a squared and engraved wooden post half-buried in a snowbank. I halted the dogs and called to Jan to show her this milepost. The lettering read: "XXVI M" on two sides, presumably carved by some roadhouse worker during a quieter off-season moment.

We took each other's picture beside the marker, wondering if this meant twenty-six miles from Black Creek Roadhouse or from Scroggie Creek. It turned out to be the only milepost we encountered on our trip.

After 12 miles, Jan and I traded off, and I put on the ever-lighter skis. For someone who had never skied before eight days ago, she was certainly doing well.

We stopped many times to investigate, snack, take photos, whatever. We are on a holiday, I reminded myself to counter an urge to rush us onward. Still, we were making excellent progress: it wasn't yet noon.

Within another mile, the snowmobile track left the old road clearance and we followed it 100 yards to a small log shelter. This was another of Peter Isaac's registered trapline cabins, a note on the door proclaimed. A row of little dog houses, relics from a time when he still used dog teams, was almost hidden by snow drifts behind the cabin.

"Lunchtime!" we both shouted simultaneously, giving ourselves license to prowl around. We ate bread and cheese, and made a little tea fire outside. The sun was washing us with tanning rays while we sat on old crates skimming through 1940s-era magazines while the dogs sprawled on the snow.

I'd followed a footpath in search of Peter's shitter [outhouse] when I came across four very naked lynx standing in a row. They were of course also very dead. My first impression was decidedly comical. Peter had removed the heads and skins from the cat-like animals, but he'd left the furry paws still attached to the carcasses. So the flesh-coloured skeletons still had fluffy white booties but no heads or clothes. They looked a rather bizarre chorus line caught in a gay death dance. I showed them to Jan – she wasn't very interested. "Not quite the Frantic Follies, eh?" I teased.

I didn't show them to the dogs, but wondered whether we should take this meat with us for their supplies. We were on the last bag of meal. We'd been out eleven days now and had food for only four more nights at most. Likely there were a dozen or so unpacked miles before the mouth of Scroggie Creek, where we'd only be a few miles from Maisy Mae

Farm upstream on the Stewart or 25 miles from the Burians at Stewart River downstream where we could surely buy some dog feed or even a sack of oats or rice. That gave us one extra day's grace at full rations.

Lynx are members of the cat family and probably have splintery, brittle bones, I figured. Dangerous for a dog. A bit like chicken bones – lynx were even reputed to taste like chicken. So I decided not to take any chances by feeding them to our crew. If we had to backtrack to Pelly Farm, we knew where they were, but otherwise we could do without. I explained my flow of logic to Jan, and she readily agreed. I didn't ask Tuk his opinion though.

When lunch was eaten, we moved on, still doing well, the air temperature barely over freezing. We'd hardly established our pace when we arrived at an old two-storey roadhouse, much like the ruined Black Creek building. Opposite it were two cabin shells. Fifty years of disuse had rendered these dwellings suitable only for firewood. We took a photo and recorded the location on the Bradleys' map as promised. This had been Alberta Roadhouse, we figured. Farther along the road we passed the remains of a corral and small shack, more relics from horse days.

So far today the dogs had been content, with not a single fight, and the toboggan had only tipped once. However the snow was now getting sticky and they couldn't quite keep up with me skiing ahead. I slowed down so they wouldn't get discouraged and Jan cheered them on, calling out their names and telling them how good they were. They took every opportunity to investigate suspicious bunny trails but I held myself back from yelling at them. One musher at a time.

'Just a few more miles' was my mantra, repeated until I believed it myself. Visions of the comfortable cabin awaiting us flourished until I knew there would be a cozy chalet with a fireplace and double bed, and lots of wood and an airtight and a clothesline with clothes-pins. Just a few more miles. We mushed on, through the poplar forest and then across a frozen muskeg swamp. Back into the forest, noticing the spruces with their saucy squirrels and chickadees.

"Are we almost there? I thought this was going to be a holiday."

"Just a few more miles, Jan, and we'll be at tonight's roadhouse. Almost there. Almost there."

Through the trees, across the creeks, swinging west to ski into the afternoon sun, we continued. Breaks were brief: a few bites of snow and a chance to catch our breath. Then up again, get up again dogs, and we'd be off again. The route was now slightly south of west.

Another short side-track took us to one of Peter's line cabins. It certainly wasn't the chalet of my dreams, so dark and dirty in its gloomy forest. Out on the main road the sun still shone – we pressed on to reach Scroggie Roadhouse and the end of Peter's trail.

Just after four p.m., we rounded a corner, went down a hill and turned right again. Above us, in glorious ruin, was the roadhouse. No bed, no cozy fireplace, nothing except a huge mess. The sod roof was on the floor under a foot of snow. Every pot and pan left from the kitchen had been shot through by bullets. All the furniture was smashed to pieces.

Somewhere our signals had gotten crossed. I was sure Peter had said there was a good cabin at Scroggie at the end of his track. Here was the loop for turning around; ahead the old road was unpacked and drifted.

"He must have meant that last line cabin, miles back," I muttered.

I circled the old building, highstepping through the knee-deep soggy snow. It was the right consistency for making snowballs but too deep and wet for walking through. My ski boots, socks and pants were soaked through and my temper rising.

"Dammit, we deserve a dry cabin!" I didn't want to look at Jan.

There was nowhere decent to camp around the roadhouse either. The forest here was mostly small poplar – no shelter with only green wood to burn. The creek water was running rust-coloured and tasted swampy. Nothing was right. It was clouding over, Peter's last cabin was miles back and uphill, the road ahead was impassable until packed and frozen, and most of our gear was damp or wet.

Trying to make the best of it, we dragged a wooden wall from the roadhouse out onto the road as a sleeping platform. Three at a time we let the dogs have a chance to explore and sniff about. Dependable old Rafferty peed on the food box and was headed for Jan when I grabbed and chained him up. Flander climbed onto the wall section with snow all over him and settled in to sleep on our sleeping bags. Tuk found the last spot still in the sunshine and lay there on his belly like a grand white lion. When their turn came, the other three headed for the hills and came back half an hour later wearing their tongues like neckties and eager for suppertime. For supposedly tired dogs, they'd discovered quite a lot of energy for playtime.

They had a long wait for their stewed crunchies because the fire wouldn't cooperate. I sawed up the few dead and half-dead poplars nearby and chopped down lots of thin green ones. With an old newspaper and thinly split kindling, I built a good starter fire and added some of the poplar. It smoked, smoked and smoked some more, but gave no heat. Only after a good ninety minutes of fussing with bits of punky fuel and wet planks from the roadhouse, did we manage to get a meal cooked. Only then did the fire really catch – when we didn't need it any more.

The meal was incredibly bad. Jan did her best to make an omelette from powdered eggs but neither of us could eat more than a few mouthfuls of the resultant rubbery frisbee. It was the only meal we didn't finish all trip. We ate canned sardines instead.

Always the experimenter, I zipped our sleeping bags together, put the wool blanket inside the double bag and pulled the tarp over us. The condensation from the tarp couldn't really do our damp bags much harm. I put on a sweater, long johns, booties and toque before crawling in; Jan was wearing her flannel bunny pyjamas, sweater and canvas parka. Fortunately the fashion police didn't patrol this territory.

For a long time we lay there on our backs, not speaking, uncomfortably conscious of the smell of our hair and skin and clothes. Near midnight we watched with cold faces exposed as the sky cleared and Northern Lights appeared centre stage o'erhead. The curtain-like sheets danced to an unheard rhythm. Reds, blues, greens flashed, rippled and faded, then reappeared with increased vigour, while a backdrop of thousands of yellow stars slowly revolved around Polaris, the pole star. Quite a heavenly presentation for two exhausted refugees from the Viking Hall of the Slain.

CHAPTER 14

STROLLING WITH MR. CASEY AND MS. MITTI

Cold again. We woke and kept shivering back to sleep until the sun rose and warmed the air a few degrees. By then it was eleven o'clock. Tonight, we agreed, we'd have to try something much better if we were to get a decent sleep. Jan wasn't any warmer than I was even though she'd monopolized the blanket masterfully. (If a woman does it, should that be *mistressfully?*)

About one, I started out on snowshoes to pack trail. Jan elected to stay by the wooden platform and do chores: re-packing the tobog-gan, mending harnesses, drying socks, airing the sleeping bags and a multitude of other duties we'd postponed until we got to the proverbial cabin-we'll-get-to-tonight.

In a few minutes I came back to change to the skis. The freeze-thaw crust on this section was too hard for me to break with my big snow-shoes. They were almost five feet long and ideal for staying on top of powdery Yukon cold winter snow. But right now I wanted to break into the snow to create a trail for the dogs and toboggan. I started out again, noting one ski boot had a cracked toe piece and might not last much longer. Jan suggested I take two dogs along to help trample the trail. After I decided Casey and Mitti would get into the least trouble, we departed to an earth-shaking clamour raised by the other dogs. This was soon drowned out by Jan's ominous "QUI-ET!!!"

The trail-breaking was hard work but quite satisfying. The dogs leapt through the snow and tunnelled after rabbit smells, and barked at ravens. I relished the break from my own barking at sled dogs, while I cleared with an axe the few trees fallen across the roadway. On the way back four hours later, I stomped the trail a bit wider and created extra wide corners to keep the toboggan from catching and tipping.

Jan had a hot fire ready – burning boards from the roadhouse – when I returned. We warmed our feet and drank tea.

"Did you miss me?" I asked.

"To tell the truth, it was great to have a break. Bet you felt the same way, right?

"Sure. It's good to break up routines, to find our balance again. Who mushes first, who feeds the dogs, who sets up a shelter – or whether we sleep without one—"

"—Jeez, you talk so much without saying much, Bruce. Let's get going."

We bundled the sleeping gear onto the toboggan, hitched the dogs and left Scroggie Roadhouse at six-thirty. My packed trail proved a few inches too narrow but the dogs were able to pull the toboggan through, ploughing a great pile of snow in front of the curl. Every hundred feet or so, we had to help the team by kicking that build-up of crusted snow off the trail so the toboggan could slide again – and create a new pile.

At seven-thirty, we camped beside the road under a huge spruce and were able to cook supper over a decent fire. I happily chopped a generous pile of boughs for insulation under our bedding.

The weird, eerie sunset dog howling interrupted our meal. We paused to watch the distorted facial expressions and listen to each dog's distinctive wailing. Some sounded so sad and mournful, like a Delta blues guitarist on a tear. Were their songs doors of perception into an inner nature, to a wolfish past?

Putting our bowls aside, Jan and I joined in.

"I enjoyed trail packing this afternoon," I said across the fire. "Just what I needed after that *holiday* yesterday. Tomorrow we should reach the Stewart and know how the river trail will be."

"Now *that* will be cause for celebration," Jan nodded.

CHAPTER 15

NOT A GOOD DAY

Friday the thirteenth. Ten days had elapsed since leaving the highway at Pelly Crossing. We'd told Three-Quarter Jon we'd take ten, at most 14, days to reach Dawson or be back in Pelly. I imagined him in his Whitehorse shop wondering about his dogs (and us) and looking at the circled days on the girlie wall calendar. I thought hard, 'We're okay, Jon,' and hoped the telepathic message got through. There were no cell phones in the Yukon in 1977.

The temperature hadn't dropped as much last night, making for a warmer sleep, but also meaning the snow crust wasn't frozen very thoroughly except in shaded areas. It was soft in any spots exposed to the sun. I snowshoed ahead and backtracked over the deep places while Jan moved the dogs forward in stages.

The first one mile was beautiful going, so encouraging, but unfortunately no indication of those to come. The road started to wind up and down the valley sides in steep ascents and soppy sun-exposed descents. The 'boys' couldn't manage unpacked sections beyond 40 feet when their initial momentum was expended.

I could hear Jan as I packed and repacked the heavy snow: "It is only 10 miles, you guys. Come on. Get up. Let's GO!" She sounded like a football cheerleader gamely encouraging perennial losers.

We were off the last 50,000:1 topographical map and never sure exactly where we were. From the small scale version it seemed only about 10 miles from the mouth of Walhalla Creek to the Stewart as the raven flies. I estimated that a raven wearing snowshoes might walk a lot farther on our winding road, especially if it stomped its route three times.

My snowshoes sank about a foot into the wet snow, collecting in the process a 10-pound load of ice and snow through the webbing and from the sides of the depression. I had to shuffle backwards to spill the snow so I could stomp it hard again before continuing with the next step. For hours it was step-step forward, shuffle back and shake off, and step-step forward again, shuffle back and shake, and so on.

Sometimes the dogs could follow that initial trail, but more often I needed to tramp back, widening the way and then walk over it for the third time in front of Iskoot.

The dogs were giving Jan a real going-over. They had been fighting, eating harnessing, going on strike, stopping on uphills or when they saw squirrels, doing anything but steady work. Iskoot was losing interest in leading so Casey had to be drafted to go first. He would always lead, albeit slowly, but would rarely pull from that position. The others were doing his share and not willingly. Jan must have been doing a few dogs' shares herself because she was stripped down to a T-shirt in the 35°F sun.

Ahead, I was having a more tranquil time, plodding and stomping alone, axe in hand, thoroughly drenched in sweat, eating snow and nibbling bits of dried meat from my pocket. I didn't mind any of this, strangely enough.

Must be something messed up in your brain, said the voices.

Sez you. I'm sure the Stewart is round the next bend, I answered optimistically.

Where a huge spruce had fallen across the road, I made a trail around as it would have taken hours to chop through the trunk. Jan set up camp there while I snowshoed on for another half-hour. It seemed most of our camp time now revolved around drying socks and wet boots, trying to do it quickly without scorching them.

Tonight we fed the dogs only two-thirds their normal ration. This was the end of two days on the unpacked section, all the time I'd allotted. I had no idea how far we were from the mouth – it felt as though we'd already gone more than far enough. We agreed that tomorrow would have to see us on the Stewart River or we'd have to turn back, and even that would be a hungry trip. Tuk, the whiner, lodged a complaint about not getting enough. He was definitely back at the top of my Eat List.

Our latest idea on sleeping arrangements proved to be the answer. We split the double bag apart into two single bags. Jan rolled herself in the wool blanket in her bag, while I zipped my heavy parka up and pulled it over me like a psych-ward straightjacket. Inside my bag and the parka, I felt alarmingly claustrophobic but toasty warm. As Jan summed up in her log: "Not a good day with dogs; good sleep though."

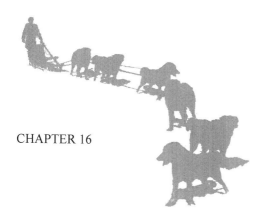

CHAPTER 16

WILL WE EVER GET THERE, DADDY?

Yes, a good warm sleep, just not nearly long enough. I woke before dawn, actually sweating. And panicking because I desperately had to pee but was trapped in my parka and bag. Think of something else, you nutcase, anything at all, I told myself while effecting a wriggling Houdini escape.

We had a hearty breakfast, frying a few extra bannock cakes in lard for lunch. The dogs were disappointed their morning beef fat ration had run out; they would have been even more alarmed to learn how depleted their meal bag was. Tonight we *had* to make it to the Stewart – or turn back.

It was an early start, about eight a.m. The first mile of mushing went well – the trail packed last night had crusted well and the toboggan rode high even though the dogs' paws were punching through at times. We frequently checked their feet for cuts and kept an eye peeled for blood spots in the snow. Mitti collected icy balls between her pads but learned to limp or bark to alert us she needed to stop and chew them clear. We were packing some canvas – currently rough-stitched into a nearly empty dog food sack – and drawstrings to make dog booties if their feet began to suffer.

Soon we were travelling along cliffs, sometimes manhandling the toboggan over bare rock then snow slides. As the old road wound in and out of steep valleys, the conditions varied from slushy puddles to deep, dense snowdrifts, and on to icy bare patches. The base of the toboggan was taking a beating on protruding stones, too many to avoid. The relatively clear stretches offered a great relief because I didn't have to pack trail there. Unfortunately they were the exception, not the rule.

Jan worked the dogs admirably, coaxing effort where there was clearly no enthusiasm. I was still stomping most sections three times. Onward. Backward. Onward.

By noon my anxiety about reaching the Stewart was making me edgy. Jan was also unnerved, exploding at the dogs, my babbling and the trail conditions. As we tried to bull the toboggan around one snowslide, the entire outfit slid sideways down the bank, dragging the two wheel dogs with it. We both lunged for it and barely managed to stop it rolling 30 feet down into the swirling brown Scroggie Creek waters below.

I looked at Jan, her feet jammed into the bank, her back straining to hold back the curl. My leg was pinned under the toboggan, its weight cutting into my calf, but the tail-end was stopped too.

"This is crazy," I said, extricating my leg slowly.

"Yep," she said, crawling up the bank warily, grasping Tuk's harness in case the toboggan decided to resume its slide. She stomped around to pack a path for the toboggan to be coaxed back onto the road. "This is *not* fun."

She's got that right, I thought. At least it hadn't fallen into the creek, dragging all the dogs and us along. I didn't say that though. Sometimes even a Pollyanna needs to shaddup.

We lifted, pushed and pried, with those miserable dogs barely keeping tension on their harnesses. Then, after a few sharp leather-mitt slaps across their heads and some mighty grunting, we tipped the toboggan onto its inside edge and muscled it along the slope until safely past the avalanche area.

Each hundred yards we negotiated was an adventure and an eternity. The dogs continued misbehaving, refusing to work and getting into another fight. Soon Jan wasn't able to keep them moving at all.

"Now what?" we said in unison. We were desperate to make distance today.

After one o'clock we gave up on the dogs and decided to work together on trail packing. We chained the dogs individually to trees beside the trail and told them to "Be good." Jan put a few goodies into her pockets for an afternoon snack and untied the skis and poles from the toboggan.

Casey and Flander, sensing we were leaving, whined to come. The others picked up on their assessment and howled like banshees as we plodded off, Jan trampling the broken crust in my wake with her skis.

The tranquillity without the team brought a total-body flush of relief. We were soon even smiling at each other. A mile down the road we could still hear the dogs crying, but felt no sympathy.

We worked steadily, always expecting to see the river around each bend. The road was on the east limit of this northward-flowing creek. On the slopes above us, clumps of last summer's grass were poking through where the snow had melted and settled from the week's hot afternoon exposures. In the shadows it was chilly and the crust was intact. Small trees barring the road I axed; larger ones we stomped detours around.

Finally at 4:30, we stopped for a rest, leaning against the cutbank and eating snow and the last soggy bannock. Jan said her ankle was 'a bit sore.' She had a tension bandage on it but was in some pain so we ate our crumbs and agreed to split up. She would return to the dogs and try to bring them up. Neither of us predicted she would have any success. She would set up camp where she could and have a fire and tea waiting for me.

"Don't be too gentle with those cheesehounds," I advised. "There's no reason they can't work."

"Maybe they are hungry."

"Maybe we are too."

She gave me the rest of the dried meat in her pack, and a smile.

"Be careful."

"You too." And she skied off.

Now I was alone, plodding on in my big snowshoes, foot after foot, sweating profusely until my down vest was soaked through. A light evening breeze was chilly in the shade so I wore my windbreaker like a cape until I was too warm again.

Always my eyes were searching the trees for tell-tale sawn stumps or axe markings. A settlement at the creek mouth would have used vast quantities of cordwood, but there were no signs.

As the road continued and the sun sank I was paying less and less attention to the trees, the brown creek, the crumbling rock bluffs, the rabbit tracks. I was worried.

I wondered when my knee would give out. On a ski trip two years ago, I strained my leg three days away from town and hadn't been able to continue without incredible pain. I holed up in a small cabin until a ski-dooer happened by and towed me out of the bush on his sled. Since then, with wall-sit exercises and better overall conditioning, the pain hadn't returned. But I hadn't snowshoed for over nine hours straight before. Or was it ten hours? I crossed my fingers and trudged on.

My mind was a mess of worries and calculations. To return to the farm might take us four days doing well. We had one night's part rations left for the dogs and four lynx carcasses back at Alberta Creek. Maybe Jan and I could eat one of those? If we'd brought a .22 rifle we could have shot some of those damned squirrels. This was certainly a bum-per year in their cycle – maybe we could snare a few when we camped overnight. Dick had reminded me that all this was someone's trapline and even squirrels were snared for their fur. I tried to estimate how many illegal squirrels six dogs and two people would need daily. Couldn't be much meat on one of the little critters. Jan and I were probably eating in the order of 3,000 to 4,000 calories per day and losing weight. The dogs had been getting five cups of racing formula dog meal and getting lighter as well.

Rabbits! But could we ever catch any since we were always on the move and too tired to set traps in the evening? The moon would be good for snaring now, although no tracks would be showing on the snowcrust. Could tell their routes by their pellets: smarten-up pills. *What are they? Try one – sure, bite into it. You'll soon smarten up, white boy.* It was a standard joke to pull on newcomers to the North. Probably no harm. Maybe even some nutrition left. Would the dogs eat rabbit pills if desperate?

I ate the last pieces of dried meat, chewing them a long time as I tromped on in thought. Tomorrow would be the fourteenth day; we would be overdue soon and missed in Dawson. I hoped they held off until we could contact somebody. Any search would be looking for us on the Yukon River...

If we got stuck, how would we last? My Eat List suddenly didn't seem so far-fetched. *Definitely start with Tuk.*

Poor Jan, what have I got her into? I'd pushed us way past any margin of safety.

Soon the sun would be down and the road still wound through more muskeg and then on along the hillsides. I was hallucinating cabins from every fallen snow-covered tree and a river valley from every side bend. My stomach was rumbling and I dreamed about having a drink of *real* orange juice. All I had left in my vest pockets was a package of mint cough drops. I scooped up a handful of loose snow and sucked it with the cough drop under my tongue. I started to giggle. Not bad at all.

Then, there it was.

The Stewart River, no mistake this time: white, flat and wide. A thousand feet across to the rounded rock bluffs on the far shore, their tops just catching the sun's last golden rays. I strained my eyes to make out a shiny, almost metallic slash across the distant snow. It had to be a snowmobile track, reflecting as silver under the pastel hurrah of sunset.

Beside the road was a lone wooden-plank skid-shack of the type mining companies use. Inside was a crude cot, table and rusty wood stove. So this was the town of Scroggie. Greetings. Glad to see you.

Immediately I started back, my heart set on bed but most of all just longing to stop. Today. Tomorrow would be okay, if Today would just mercifully end. Damn, I was tired.

On the slow march back I didn't do much to improve our trail. It was all I could do to keep my bowlegged legs moving. My tips caught whenever I shuffled, and I fell. There was no rest for screaming thighs and sore shins – you can't drag your feet in snowshoes unless the way is flat and hard-packed.

My watch showed after 8 now, almost seven hours from where Jan was with the dogs. The way back would be much faster so I might be there at midnight or maybe even eleven. Only four hours. Or three!

Nothing to it, I repeated to myself. I've only broken trail for twelve miles. And I'm hardly tired.

Not tired. *Exhausted.*

The sky's light was waining. I chewed the last mint cough drop, forgetting to suck it with snow and immediately regretting the lost treat. I checked every pocket again but there really wasn't any more dried meat, and the mint package was very empty. I licked the liner. Then I made a whistle with it and screeched at the trees. "Hey-ay!" I yelled and screeched it again. No sense being unhappy about this. *No sense?* Indeed.

I finally halted but didn't dare sit down. I watched the stars coming out and rubbed snow on my neck to wake up. Then far away behind me I heard a snapping sound. Probably a whiskey jack, I thought – it is always the smallest of critters who make the most noise – and plodded on, not worrying about trail-packing, just moving, lifting one snowshoe at a time, keeping the tips up. Whiskey jack, camp robber, Canada gray jay. Indians say each whiskey jack is the reincarnation of a sourdough gold miner, always hungry, desperate, begging for food scraps. Or it is Wee-sah-ka-chak, the trickster, a creature who helped create the world. He flaunts and fakes, and is not to be trusted. Maybe both. Pick a story. *Whatever works for you, white boy. What are you doing out here anyway?*

Fantastical shapes formed from the bushes and watched me stumble by. I didn't stop to see if they were really bushes; it didn't matter.

After an hour, I reached the place where Jan had turned back. "Three hours forward and one coming back so far," I mumbled aloud. "Maybe I'll make it there by eleven after all."

Behind me was a very soft thud, like a foot stomping in the snow and then, another.

I looked around but all was clear on the road and all was still and black in the shadows. Absolute silence.

The bush is never totally quiet. You're just not hearing outside of the confusion in your head. Let your mind be still.

Okay, sure, whatever you say. But only two hours further and I can lie down.

CHAPTER 17

JAN ALONE

Skiing slowly and favouring her weak ankle only a little, Jan made her way steadily back toward the dogs. The air was becoming noticeably chillier as the sun moved lower in the late afternoon sky.

It's almost evening now, time when sane people are sitting down at chairs and a table to eat a meal cooked on an electric stove, she thought. They are warm and relaxed; none of them have wet feet. They sip wine and talk about art or their friends – anything but sled dogs. Let's see now, which wine would that be?

Partway down a long downhill stretch coming off a bench was the huge fallen tree blocking the road. We'd stomped a trail around it earlier. There were sheltered, dry spots under any one of the five mature spruces in the clump of forest that once hosted this fallen evergreen. She made a mental note of this place as she crawled over the obstruction and continued on her way.

It was two hours before she arrived.

The dogs were quiet until Jan was almost on them. Tuk was lying loose near the toboggan and ran up to her, wagging his proud tail.

"What are you doing loose, stupid?" Jan said, then saw the broken snap still attached to his collar.

Tuk then headed for Rafferty. Rafferty looked frantic and peed on his own front legs. Jan caught up to Tuk and smacked him with a ski pole. It was effective – he cowered on the ground, then followed obediently when Jan skied to the toboggan. "Sit." He sat in the snow.

She sat on the toboggan.

"Hello, boys. Hello, Mitti."

They responded in a chorus of whines and whimpers and yawns. Tails flopped curiously while Jan took off the skis and tied them and the ski poles onto the toboggan. First she harnessed Tuk, then the others, wading through the knee-deep snow to unchain each one. Rafferty was last.

Young Iskoot was in lead, Casey next. She called, "Hike," heaved against the handlebars to break out the base, and away they went.

When Casey checked one too many critter crossings, stopping progress, she wacked him with a ski pole. That was effective. No need to yell, they knew she was serious.

The temperature was back below freezing and her ski tracks had already started to harden. The packing was enough for the dogs and toboggan; they mushed steadily over the crackling ice crystals.

The sunset was a deep golden, then a dying pink and soon the stars were out to light the grey and white world below. A dozen times the sled halted at a detour or steep hill, but there was no one to help. Alone, Jan muscled and willed the load around and onward.

Just after nine, they reached the fallen tree. Beyond exhaustion, she still had dogs to chain, camp to set, wood to gather, a fire to start, dog food to dish out, human food to prepare.

The dogs would have to wait. First she carried some people food and pans to a flat spot under the biggest spruce. Snapping off squaw branches from beside her, she knelt down and made a small pile of dry tinder. When that was lit, she added increasingly larger branches, and snugged a pot of snow against the fire. Rocking on her heels, face flushed with heat while her wet feet ached with cold and fatigue, she wondered where she'd find the energy to keep going.

Casey whined. *Miserable bugger, just wait. Jeez, I am SO tired.*

He whined again.

It was a greeting to his owner, barely mobile, stumbling up the trail and now half-crawling, half-falling over the downed tree.

I patted Casey and Iskoot, at their nests beside the trail, then gingerly parked my butt on the toboggan curl to untie the snowshoe harnesses. Stooped and woozy, I made my way to the fire and leaned against the tree.

"I thought you were angels," I said at last. "I've been to the Stewart. It's frozen clear across. There's a skidoo trail and... Thank God you're here!"

The dogs were perturbed by the meagre rations they were served. Tomorrow night they'd get even less, but we would be closer to getting more supplies.

The two humans ate their rice and mung beans slowly, savouring the nourishment, so relieved to be camped. We had no problem sleeping soundly.

CHAPTER 18

COOKIES FOR TUK

I wriggled halfway out of my sleeping bag and looked around. The sun was up but not yet shining on our sheltered position. I fished through the bundle of clothes that had served as my pillow until I found my watch. It was 6:30.

The dogs I could see were asleep except Mitti who was peacefully grooming herself. I started breaking dead branches to make a fire and she lifted her brown eyes in my direction, wagging her tail cautiously.

"Good morning, Mitti!" I whispered back.

She wagged happily, then went back to her chores. So did I.

An hour later, I woke Jan for breakfast in bed. She was perturbed I hadn't woken her earlier to 'do her share' but without question she had earned a bit of extra rest. Too bad there wasn't more variety to select from. Our morning supplies were down to good old bannock/pancakes, a dollop of peanut butter and black tea.

As we harnessed the dogs, I noticed a new ache in my ankle.

"Probably from thirteen hours of snowshoeing yesterday, most of it breaking trail," diagnosed Dr. Jan as she wrapped it tightly in a tension bandage.

With luck, there would be no call for snowshoeing today so the ligaments or whatever inside bits would have a chance to recover.

"I'm glad my knee has held out this long," I admitted. "How's your ankle?"

"Okay for now," she said. "I can do my bit."

None of the dogs were limping or visibly injured – except Tuk and Rafferty who had small open cuts from their ongoing vendetta. Tuk had lost so often his face looked like an inept boxer's, but everything was healing fine with no sign of infection. John Tapsell had given us some antibiotic powder that I'd dusted on Rafferty's leg wound just after we left Pelly Crossing. That cut was now almost healed closed. Unlike human wounds, dogs' cuts don't scab over; instead the hole stays open until hide – fur and all – gradually grows in from the edges. A little bleeding flushes the wound and an occasional tongue wipe keeps it clear of dirt.

The overnight freeze had done its trick, providing us a beautiful crust to move on. Jan and I took turns running ahead to keep warm and be the lead dog's bait. I'd sprint in my pac boots until winded, then lean over to pant and suck in the cold air until Jan and the dogs caught up. Then she ran while I rode and watched the scenery.

We hadn't gone far when Jan abruptly stopped and knelt on the trail. I whoa-ed the team and walked up.

"What kind of tracks are these?" she asked. "I've been seeing them for a ways now."

On top of last night's snowshoe imprints were newer marks. They'd been made very soon after, before my track froze and solidified. Half again as big across as Rafferty's pawprints and the same basic shape, these had to be wolf.

"I *thought* something was following me back, Jan," I said. "I heard footfalls. This was one very big, bad wolf."

"Double big is right." Her eyes were saucers and she wasn't smiling. "And maybe he wasn't alone," she added, pointing to other less-distinct prints.

Why the wolf didn't jump me in the dark was a puzzle; it would've taken very little effort to knock me over. We knew the tracks hadn't followed me right to camp, and decided a lone wolf might have been put off by so many dog scents unless it was very hungry. That seemed to reassure Jan. I'd been far more worried about bumping into a wolverine in the dark.

The long hours of yesterday's effort were paying off now as we whizzed along, covering the distance in a fraction of the time. Our spirits were high. The sun was showing promise of a hot afternoon. Perhaps we could spend it lounging around at Maisy Mae Creek not far upriver on the far shore of the Stewart. There was supposed to be some sort of farm or at least people living there, I mused as I bounced along on the toboggan tail. And from there, we could expect snowmachine-packed trails and mining roads leading to the Klondike River headwaters and on to Dawson City.

Twenty minutes later, and almost to the creek mouth, I was running ahead again and had left the others behind. I stopped to wait, listening for sounds of a dog fight then, hearing none, figured the delay was most likely a broken harness. Looking around, I was surprised to spot a log cabin on the opposite side of the creek. It was well camouflaged under snow but from what I could make out, it was in good shape.

Tapped with a pole, the creek ice sounded solid enough, so I scampered across and scrambled up the far bank. Glancing back, I noticed water filling my last bootprint. "Guess I'll figure out how to get back *after* checking the cabin," I muttered to no one. "Might as well explore while I'm here."

The cabin might have been a telegraph station; there were thick wires attached to glass insulators on a wooden mast pegged to one wall. An old sled had been left nearby under the eaves, its boards rotted and the metal runners deeply pitted with rust. It was heavy to lift, even empty, with all those metal bolts and braces.

The door wasn't locked, just partially blocked with snow, so I was able to peek inside. There was an intact stove, table and chairs, utensils and pots and pans, books on shelves; it hadn't been ransacked by bears or humans. Perhaps its location had saved it from notice.

When Jan arrived opposite with the dogs, I called her over. She tested the ice more carefully and determined the water was flowing over solid ice so it was entirely safe to cross even the last part. She instructed the dogs to take a break and sleep in the sun.

Together we explored the interior, leafing through old magazines and books, trying to imagine living here. In the back room was the bed, the straw mattress surprisingly not yet attacked by mice. "This cabin must have a weasel, too, to eat any mice," I commented, and went back outside to enjoy the sun.

Jan was announcing crazy articles in the magazines while I examined the log construction workmanship. There was a pause in Jan's banter and she appeared in the doorway with a small cardboard canister with a tight metal cap.

"Wouldn't this make a good dope stash?" she joked and handed it to me. It was about two-and-a-half inches in diameter, an inch high, with 'Gin Pills for the Kidneys' printed in garish lettering on the label. It rattled when shaken.

"Sure would," I replied and twisted off the lid. I stepped out into the direct sunshine to examine the contents. "Probably seventy-year-old gin pills in here. Whatever gin pills are."

It was gold. Small nuggets of placer gold.

I poured them out very carefully into my palm and showed Jan. "I think this is gold, Jan."

She looked at the contents with sudden interest, poking with a cautious finger, turning them over. Then she broke into a grand smile and shouted, "G-O-L-D!"

She was ecstatic. "Gold! Gold!" she kept shouting and dancing around. "I found gold!"

I skipped across the creek and told the dogs who pretended to know what was happening and wagged their tails. Then I unpacked the camera and hurried back to Janet.

She posed for a picture, then continued bouncing up and down. Abruptly she stopped. "Maybe there's more," she exclaimed and dashed back inside.

We checked every corner, every container, but no more luck. The gin pills canister Jan discovered had been sitting out on the counter beside the bed, not hidden at all. We wondered why it had been abandoned. Who would leave their stash behind?

"A mystery indeed!" Jan proclaimed. "No one has been in this cabin for decades probably."

Her feet weren't touching the ground for hours afterward. Every

Gin Pills for the Kidneys said the cannister's label. But inside was a very different cure that 40,000 prospectors were seeking in 1898.

time we stopped, she unpacked her treasure from its secure place and looked at it again. "I can't believe it. I can't believe it."

Before noon we were at the Stewart River. We stomped back and forth between the creek mouth and the snowmobile track to pack a trail for the dogs. In places, there was an inch of water under the snow, but when I chopped with my axe to test ice thickness I quit after a solid eight inches.

The dogs were a little perturbed about the water but I grabbed Iskoot's harness and, with Jan shouting, "Come on, boys!" they quickly splashed through it and up onto the track.

As with much of Danny's trail, this track sat above adjacent snow levels. It had been hard-packed all winter while surrounding areas had lost some of their loose snow cover to blowing winds and recent thawing.

From our big map, it appear there should be a roadway – actually a continuation of the overland stage road – starting on the north shore and running perhaps four miles east to Maisy Mae Creek. Indeed there was an old snowmobile trace forking off, so we followed that until we were foundering in thigh-deep snow. We wrestled the toboggan and dogs another hundred yards to the shore and found the start of the road, but it was totally bare of snow the first 100 feet.

I scouted ahead and found more bare patches before it started uphill. Not very promising, this. We could either yank the toboggan a few feet at a time through the muddy patches and hope for no deep snow, or turn around and head downstream for the Burian homestead at the old Steward Island townsite where this river joined the Yukon. We weren't sure there was anyone wintering this year at Maisy Mae, but were absolutely certain someone would be at Stewart Island. The Burian family had lived there for generations and operated a store for local trappers and summer canoe tourists. The packed trail heading in that direction looked very tempting. It was about 25 miles to the confluence. The vote was two for, none against, with six abstentions. We turned around and headed back to the snowmachine trail.

Soon we were mushing toward the Yukon, passing over tracks that must have been made earlier today. It felt odd, a sign of company in this vast wilderness after a week alone together. I looked down at the imprints again and felt a weight lifted from my shoulders.

"Yahooooo!" I yelled and waved my arms about.

"What did you find?" the golden girl asked.

"This is like a highway! People drive on this all the time. To Dawson and back. Someone was here – two machines, I think – this morning. It is going to be like a sidewalk all the way to Dawson. We've just about made it."

"Yeah? I hope this isn't going to be another *holiday* like last time," she smiled.

"No. Just like this. A snow-covered sidewalk for one hundred miles."

For the first few miles, the trail kept to the thick shelf ice along the south cliffs, where the shade had kept the snow frozen. By late afternoon, though, we were weaving through sloughs and near islands, fully exposed to the sun. The reflection off this much river surface was dazzling, the glare near blinding with each crystal of ice acting as a mirror. We wore our sunglasses and felt the reflected rays baking our exposed skin. The expanses of snow were shimmering with heat waves.

We draped wet socks and mitts over the load on the toboggan, dangling long johns and the blue bunny suit from the ends of the snowshoes. Our outfit resembled a mobile used car lot with everything flapping like so many flags.

Each patch of open water we passed vividly illustrated the ever-present danger of falling through the ice. Could the person going ahead drag a long enough safety rope for the musher to grab? But we didn't have two or three hundred feet of rope. And even if we did, a trailing rope would have snagged in cracks and become tangled around ice blocks. Carrying a long pole wasn't practical either. A sturdy enough length of wood would be unwieldy and heavy, exhausting to pack for hours. Surely, we rationalized, simply being on skis was spreading the lead person's weight, and the best safety rested in paying close attention to the contours and colour of the river's surface. Sunken, darker places were a definite no-go.

Past Barker Creek, then Telford Creek, and the going was getting too slushy. The dogs' paws were punching through the crust at times, as were the musher's boots if walking behind. We decided to camp early and do the remaining fifteen miles tomorrow morning while everything would be crisp. This would give us a chance to dry socks and fix harnessing and have a leisurely supper. The effects of yesterday's exertions were being felt as well.

With my watch saying four o'clock, we looked forward to having lots of time. But within two hours it was nearly dark, so my watch must have been fatigued too. I guesstimated and re-set it for eight-thirty.

Again we had rice and beans, eating while watching the sun set toward Stewart Island. I felt more relaxed than I had in ages.

"I wouldn't bring rice on any future trips," Jan said. "Takes too much time to cook. Better to just bring beans."

"Future trips? Hasn't this cured you of winter camping?"

"Oh, well, maybe someday I'd go on another trip. But with better dogs. And not a rush. This is plain nuts."

In the dusk, I fed the dogs a final cup and a half of dog meal and tried to divide the dust and crumbs fairly. The looks of horror and indignation would have moved a lesser man to tears. But tomorrow, I figured, they could eat a feast from Rudy Burian's store.

"Just get us there, fellas. And if Burians can't sell us some dog food, oats or rice, Tuk," I promised, "I'll buy you your own private bag of cookies."

CHAPTER 19

ALMOST, ALWAYS ALMOST

When the sun rose at 5:30 a.m., we were already on the move. The last of our coffee and a rather raw bannock were sloshing wildly in my stomach as I stood against the handlebars and slapped my mitts together to warm my fingers against the 24°F air. Jan was skiing, easily keeping well ahead.

The dogs weren't too energetic. They hadn't wanted to wake up in the pre-dawn glow, and weren't any more interested in travelling now. I stepped off the tail every few hundred yards and jogged behind to make their work easier, although there was very little toboggan friction on the crisp trail surface. The pace the dogs fell into was faster than my walk but slower than a run – dog-walk you could call it. They look half asleep but they'll wake up when they smell the other dogs at Burians, I thought and turned my attention to the growing sunrise behind us. This summer, I promised myself, I'll come back and see this river properly, in a canoe – a more civilized way to travel. Maybe invite my parents for a holiday, show them this territory I was fixated on.

We were so looking forward to an early arrival at Stewart Island. It was only about 10 miles more in a straight map line. Of the dozen pairs of socks we'd brought, Jan was wearing the only totally dry pair. The rest were in various degrees of dampness and ruin. Fortunately not all the holes and tears matched up, so by wearing four random socks – two on each foot, of course – I was able to keep my feet adequately covered. This afternoon, though, we could dry and mend the lot, in a real cabin.

Heading down a slough, the trail abruptly ran out of snow. There was a mud patch with shallow water running along it. Yesterday's machine tracks ran clearly across the mud and back on more snow 20 yards beyond. But those snowmachines were probably going 30 miles an hour on early morning frozen muck. It was no longer frozen.

We stopped. What now? Do we make wheels from something or pole rollers? Go back to the head of this slough and pack a trail around? But that might take hours. I wanted to stick to the track the river people followed, for they would surely know the safest spots.

First we tried to mush right across. No luck. I yelled at the dogs and threatened to make poodle food from their sorry carcasses but they couldn't budge the toboggan. Jan and I crouched low and pushed as hard as we could, but it still wouldn't budge. The suction in the soft mud held it fast.

Jan had an idea. Why not try pushing the toboggan through the shallow water? After trying so hard to avoid water, it seemed crazy to find ourselves prying the toboggan, jimmying it sideways first one end, then the other, right into the icy flow – even if it was only two inches deep here.

Jan called to the dogs – and away they went! She splashed through the deeper water beside Iskoot, holding his harness so he couldn't turn onto the muddy shore. He soon forgot his concern and devoted his full attention to biting at her sleeve as he ran. Moments later, with a mighty heave, we hauled the sopping toboggan back onto a snow trail and sat down to empty our boots. The dogs lay down to lick their paws dry.

"So much for dry socks," Jan muttered, wringing out her socks.

"All part of a holiday," I quipped. "A morning dip. Supposed to be good for the constitution."

"A cabin will be better for this girl's constitution," Jan sighed. "Let's go."

We followed the trail another mile along the slough as the island crowded closer to the main shore and the banks on both sides became steeper. The tall evergreen forest had shaded the trail for the last stretches and kept it frozen, but soon the noonday sun would be taking its toll. We were glad of the early start today.

Then we stopped again. There was no mud this time, only water. I splashed across the 15-foot gap, finding about six inches depth most of the way, twelve inches in spots. Now what? Build a boat? Carry each item? We had another conference and Jan decided it was my turn for a bright idea.

So I took the axe, climbed the bank and started murdering trees. It made me feel a whole lot better and I yelled back that I was building an ark for the next great flood. She could carry the camera and sleeping bags across if she didn't trust my engineering.

The dogs lay calmly by the toboggan, watching with tilted heads and raised eyebrows as I dragged de-limbed poplars down the bank, wallowing up to my waist in the snow drifts. I laid three tree trunks parallel in the water, forming a running surface for the toboggan, and explained my plan to Jan and the dogs. She would stay on one side of the toboggan and I'd stay on the other, so we could steady it on its poplar runway. The dogs' assignment was to run across, through the water, just beside my construction marvel.

But the dogs refused to enter the water. So Jan had to push Iskoot first, and soon all the dogs were splashing across nowhere near the poplars and dragging, despite my best efforts, the toboggan into deeper water.

"Quick, keep them going across!" I yelled and Jan ran to the other side, calling them to follow. I pushed from behind and the toboggan was dragged, pushed and no doubt partly floated across and then up onto the continuation of the track.

Again we sat down to wring out socks, wondering just what else we would have to do today. Jan couldn't find her sunglasses when we were ready to leave, and despite a thorough search of every pocket, the toboggan, the snow, and then in the water and on the other side, we came up with no trace.

"Too bad. They were definitely trend setting," I said.

"Yep, could have made me a star. Could have been famous."

We would switch off wearing mine from here on. Maybe we'd make some slit eye protection like the Inuit wear – when we got to Burians.

The track wound on through slough after slough, along cliffs and sometimes right down the centre of the Stewart. It was cloudless and calm; we were burning up as though it was a desert. The dogs were panting, drooping their tongues sorrowfully and flopping down at the slightest delay. Casey was constantly chewing the traces so we kept slapping his mouth and re-tying them with scraps of poly rope. Soon there were so many loose ends it looked as if he was decorated in pompoms, but he kept gnawing. I considered peeing on the new ropes to make them unsavoury, but then decided the salts would merely lure him on.

The dogs decided they weren't going to pull the toboggan *plus* a musher in the sticky snow, so I loped along behind, sometimes stopping to admire an ice formation or rock face, letting the dogs go well ahead before running to catch up. Where the crust would bear it, I'd run faster and pass the dogs just to see their puzzled looks as they counted to two and realized there was no human steering the toboggan.

High overhead we could see eagles flying. Two were small; the other four had white heads. Their nests must be high on the bluffs behind Stewart Island. It was good to see we were getting closer because Flander was starting to act up now in this heat.

As we began to veer off to the right of the maze of islands and bars, I pointed out the Yukon River valley and Shamrock Dome on the opposite shore, promising Jan: "We aren't far now."

Our single track abruptly branched, then branched again, and again – until the river seemed a scribble of tracks, some old ones which headed for now-open channels and others which seemed like recent detours. One even toured around a small island and came right back; maybe that was a trapline loop. We followed what we figured were the freshest markings but had to abandon them where they went through some evil-looking open water. Maybe it was overflow, but it sure looked black. Eventually we thought we had the right track but were headed northward along the cliffs, well back off the main Yukon River channel that Stewart Island faced.

Jan was getting edgy too.

"Aren't we ever going to get there?" she sighed, and I was wondering the same thing myself.

"What if we miss it?" she persisted. "Where's the next place anyone lives?"

I told her 20 miles and she began to look frightened.

We had to go farther west through these islands, and we had to go soon because the crust was disappearing. We'd soon be foundering in four inches of mushy corn snow.

The freshest tracks now forked off the main trail and climbed a dirt bank, heading west. It seemed the right direction. We decided to try it but the toboggan jerked to a halt on the first yard of dry ground. The dogs promptly lay down, feigning exhaustion. I walked to the top of the bank to see if it would get any worse and found the next 30 feet was bare grass.

Behind me, an abrupt outbreak of barking from the recently infirmed meant a squirrel was somewhere about. I told them to 'cool it,' and listened carefully. Our dogs' clamour bounced off the high cliffs behind us but not all the echoes stopped. Burian dogs had heard us. The sound was due west. Then a couple of rifle shots faintly echoed off the cliffs too.

The squirrel jumped to a new tree and the commotion started again. But this time I was bowled over by Iskoot, Flander, Rafferty and Mitti as they stampeded over me in hot pursuit, all still harnessed together. We ended in a heap on the grass with Iskoot and Flander fighting on my chest. With a few sharp elbows and a knee to any ribs that presented themselves, I managed to divide the combatants at least as far as the harnessing would allow. Below us, Casey, who had caused the problem by eating through Mitti's traces, was still linked to Tuk who was fastened to the toboggan.

Exasperated and near to panic, I dragged the others back down the bank, and slapped Casey. Tuk lay down immediately and then looked surprised I'd not slapped him too.

"Sonofabitch! Why the hell does everything have to go wrong all the time? Bastard!" and on and on I yelled.

When Jan asked, "What do you want me to do?" I glared at her, until I caught myself and stopped. Then she stared at me for a while until she felt better.

She went ahead on this island pathway on her skis over the grass, snow and dirt patches into the forest to scout it out. After a few minutes she reported it seemed to "just go along this island." There were more bare patches than snow.

So, after scrounging yet another two lengths of rope, we repaired Mitti's traces, adding yet another yellow poly pompom knot, and turned the dogs and toboggan around to try another route.

We had followed the next fork perhaps a hundred yards including a tricky muddy spot, when we had to quit. The trail ended at the edge of a very open, very deep, flowing channel, spanning from island to island. This wasn't the way either.

I hadn't known exactly why I had been nursing my ski boots with the cracked toe ready to fall apart, by letting Jan do all of today's skiing, but I'd had a hunch I might need them one special last time. This must be it. I was getting fed up with not being there. We all were.

I wrung out my socks, laced on the flimsy boots and skied back, past the squirrel turn-off, out onto the calligraphy of tracks and headed west. If I could get to Burians', surely someone there could tell me the shortest trail to take back to below the cliffs.

With skis I felt fairly safe on the ice – my weight was well distributed and I could travel quickly. The crust remaining on even the faintest old snowmobile track should hold me if I kept moving.

At each grey mushy patch, I jabbed down with my ski poles to sound for solid ice under the overflow and then kept on going. Trails branched off to my right, heading into the many sloughs and some joined in from the left, possibly from up the Yukon River.

I followed the paths as far west as possible and kept south of the biggest mass of islands until I was staring out over the half-mile wide main channel of the Yukon itself. The main current, not far from where I stood, was open and roaring, its waters cutting right up to Stewart Island's western bank. So much for my hopes of skiing up to the Burians' front door.

I didn't want to chance any more wrong turns in the sloughs behind the old settlement, so I took off the skis and started overland, crawling over frozen poplars, wading through knee-deep slush and fighting rose bushes, but keeping parallel to the Yukon so I wouldn't miss their home.

A half-mile later I was drenched in sweat, covered in scratches and dirt and bits of bark, looking down at the now completely torn toe piece on my ski boot, and not quite believing I was there. I dropped my poles and skis in a heap beside the big house.

"Where did you come from?" was Mrs. Burian's first question. But I wondered if she really meant, "We'd given up on you long ago."

The territory's moccasin telegraph had been at work. A government surveyor had heard from someone in Dawson about our plans. When he visited here 10 days ago aboard a helicopter, he'd passed on the news. The Burians, however, assumed I must have abandoned the trip and headed back to Pelly Crossing.

I explained I'd not quite made it here in total yet, because my partner and dog team were still back by the cliffs. "Which trail does one take? We are sorta lost."

She asked her son Ivan, who'd just come outside, to drive me back on his snowmachine. In a few minutes we were roaring through the forest, across sloughs, more islands and finally after about a mile, we popped out at the squirrel turn-off.

"Now which way are they?" Ivan asked over the motor's roar, and I pointed left.

Jan had filled a page in her notebook with her unique shorthand while I was gone:

"Weather hot & clear all day til now bummer. We Rn't sure how 2 get 2 Burians can hear dogs wailing. Ours listen don't answer. Bruce gone on skis 2 check things out. I & dogs R staked out in ft. of open trail. pleasant sound of water bad news 4 us. Feet soaked from crossing slough this morning encouraged until heard shooting, oh no wrong island some one is just hunting & will go off & we will never see them. feet freezing. overcast. can hear ski-doo good news? distant—"

Ivan was a real gentleman for not howling with laughter or mockery when he saw our ensemble. The dogs looked dead, their harnesses a shamble of cords, straps and poly rope, the toboggan on its last splinters of base, Janet and I sunburnt and filthy. Ours was a long ways from the trapping outfits he'd grown up around. He quietly helped us turn the team around as if we were just another bush neighbour visiting, and graciously offered Jan the back of his snowmobile to ride.

With Jan disappearing with this stranger, the dogs became quite alarmed and actually ran in pursuit. Ivan packed a short detour around the barren 'squirrel' approach so we could stay on the snow, and helped us lift the toboggan out of the deep snow when I overshot the corner.

Then we were off again, crashing through the forest, scrambling across bare patches and bouncing off snow banks, the dogs all running

Following the snowmobile trails beside open water. There was no rest from our worries about falling through the ice.

with their tongues flapping, Iskoot desperate to catch up to Jan. It was all I could do to keep the toboggan upright and hang on as I enjoyed the wild ride.

Ivan slowed every hundred yards to let the dogs almost catch up before he roared off, with Jan yelling, "Come on, Iskoot! Come on!"

And so we arrived at the Stewart Island townsite, looking almost like a reasonably fit team to the small crowd who'd heard the commotion and gathered to be entertained.

CHAPTER 20

RECUPERATING WITH COOKIES, BUT NONE FOR TUK

One of the first gold strikes in the Yukon Territory was in 1884 up the Stewart River. With 100 men reportedly working the river's sand and gravel bars within two years, Jack McQuesten opportunely established a trading post on the largest island at the confluence with the Yukon River. His settlement became known as Stewart River.

In 1896, Keish, a Tahltan-Tagish Indian also known as 'Skookum Jim' Mason, panned nuggets from Rabbit Creek in the Klondike River watershed, and the territory would never be the same again. Skookum Jim and his companions George Carmack and Dawson Charlie became rich and world famous, Rabbit Creek was re-christened Bonanza Creek and 40,000 men stampeded in from every corner of the world, rushing past Stewart River, headed for a new townsite near the strike called Dawson City. One man reported to have wintered at Stewart River en route to the Klondike gold fields was the storyteller, Jack London. In 1898, the Mounted Police established a post on the island, and four years later a post office was opened.

Soon there was a telegraph office on the shore opposite the island. Margaret Shand, who operated a roadhouse at Stewart River, became known as the 'Little Mother of the North.' [In that era, being called a little mother was a compliment, trust me on that.] The town developed into an important transfer point for ore brought on steamboats down the Stewart from the silver mines near Mayo Landing. The ore was then taken on larger boats up to Whitehorse, from where it went by train to the Alaska coast for shipping to smelters in the South.

Eventually, with the construction in the 1950s of all-weather roads to carry the ore, and as fur prices declined so that trapping was uneconomical, the island community dwindled. By the 1970s only one family remained. Rudy and Yvonne Burian stayed to raise their children, trapping, operating the post office and trading post, and freighting cargo on the river.

The group watching our arrival was the total population of Stewart River now: Rudy and Yvonne, son Ivan who had guided us, the other son Robin and his lady RoseMary, plus their guest, Cybil Britton. They greeted us warmly and showed us where we could chain the dogs and which guest cabin we could rent. Quite politely no one mentioned how scruffy we looked.

Mrs. Burian invited us to join them for supper, saying, "It's ready now," so we dashed off to make ourselves more presentable. I was delighted to find a woodbox full of split kindling and stacks of firewood on the porch. While Jan brushed her hair and washed over a basin, I lit a fire in the airtight heater so the cabin would be warm when we got back. I wondered what could be done to make myself 'more presentable' too. After recycling the least dirty shirt from the pack and wiping my face, I was still puzzled about footwear. I couldn't wear boots into their house and all the socks were sopping wet and rather odiferous. Finally I wrung out my quilted boot liners and wore them hoping no one would notice the wet footprints.

Mrs. Burian had the good china out and served mooseburgers and tomato macaroni with creamed cabbage. I was starved and almost ate my plate before the food was passed my way. Everyone was being so pleasant and restrained while I was merrily wolfing the last of my seconds and reaching for a third helping when Jan took my plate away!

Instantly I understood exactly how Tuk felt when the dog food ran out. I almost stabbed her hand with my fork until I looked up and saw everyone else had finished and they were clearing the table for dessert.

I scarfed down two bowls of bread pudding before it disappeared too, and would have eaten more but had to slow down to answer questions now and then. I was just getting into second eating gear when the meal was over and tea served.

"Pssst," Jan was nudging me. "Use your saucer," she whispered and I realized it wasn't a mug but a teacup.

I glanced around and was relieved that Rudy was leaning an elbow on the table. Maybe he was just doing that to make me feel less clumsy.

I nudged Jan back and suggested we reveal her secret. She agreed and passed the gin pills container to Rudy, calmly saying, "Look what we found at Scroggie."

To our great delight, Rudy took only a quick glance and dismissed the contents as crumbled pills. Ivan had a look next and said to his dad, "I think you'd better put your glasses on. This is gold."

Ivan weighed the find on a scale and determined it to be one-and-a-quarter pennyweights. At twenty pennyweights per ounce, the value was only about ten dollars – a bit more to a jeweller who could make it into nugget jewellery to sell to tourists, Robin explained. To the three men, the distinctive pale colour of the nuggets suggested an origin of either Brewer or Scroggie creeks.

For our benefit, the Burians pieced together who had lived in the Scroggie cabin. A roadhouse had been run by Joe Braga but was closed in 1927. Since then, various people had lived on the creek, mining and trapping. Mrs. Burian told us about one miner on Scroggie who had whittled a pair of birch skis for a spring visit to Stewart. He skied, as we had, on the icy crust, but by the time he reached Stewart Island, the skis had worn right out. We told her our set of skis was also precariously thin.

In the 1940s and early '50s, Jan's 'gold cabin' belonged to Bill Mason and later to Monty Velge. No one had lived there since, so the gold stash had been abandoned for over 20 years.

While the others discussed life on the river, Rudy and I slipped over to the store building where I bought some supplies for us and, more importantly, for the dogs. Two years ago Rudy had given up on dogs himself and switched to a 'power-toboggan' but luckily for us he still had two bags of dogmeal remaining which he sold me at the old price. The transaction consumed the last of our money and more; I promised to send him the $3.65 I'd overspent. Rudy just smiled. I wasn't the first traveller the Burians had rescued in their many years here, and I knew there would be others as long as people insist of making risky, ill-planned trips like ours.

Thus Tuk had to be satisfied with Buckerfield's meal instead of cookies. He made no complaints when I walked around in the dark and gave each pooch a late dry supper. I certainly had no complaints either. My belly was over-full and there was no reason to wake early in the morning. What a relief.

The 'day of rest' was therapeutic beyond measure. We slept late and then visited with Cybil in her adjacent tourist cabin where she was baking cookies. She'd produced dozens and said those we didn't eat now could be taken with us.

Cybil had come up to Stewart River from Dawson, about 80 miles, mushing a rented team herself close on the heels of Gerry Couture and his main team. It was Cybil's first experience running dogs as she lives in Philadelphia. The trip upriver had taken two days with light sleighs. Three days later she was still emotionally high about it.

We were impressed with that pace but "that was nothing – Cowboy made it in eight hours," she'd been told. Apparently on crisp, mid-winter packed snow, Larry Smith had coaxed nine dogs to average over ten miles per hour, pausing only for two short rests. That contrasted sharply with the fifteen miles in eight hours our dogs had managed yesterday, even if the conditions were more suited to swimming than mushing.

Jan and Cybil formed an immediate bond, obviously anxious to talk 'as girls' together, so I excused myself and wandered outside.

Rudy was sitting on a bench staring out across the Yukon. I sat beside him and thanked him again for renting us a cabin so we could rest up. "We were all pretty exhausted," I said.

"Those dogs of yours were not as tired yesterday as you believed," he said matter-of-factly, "or they wouldn't have been so noisy during the night."

The crew, especially Tuk, were just too vocal for 'well worked' dogs apparently. They'd been playing us.

Neither Jan nor I were tired so we stayed up chatting with Cybil and telling old camping stories until after midnight. While eating more of those cookies and drinking gallons of tea, we re-packed the toboggan and repaired harnesses, using borrowed pliers. We finished the last preparations just before two o'clock.

The 'plan' was to be up early to catch the crust – a 5 a.m. start. That left less than three hours to sleep but we could sleep in the afternoon sun somewhere. Tomorrow we'd be out on the Yukon River ice trail, bound for Dawson, only 80 miles away.

And we wouldn't be carrying much extra load: there was hardly a cookie left.

CHAPTER 21

BRIAN'S ROADHOUSE

I lit the kerosene lamp and made us each a sandwich of cold bannock with some jelly and yesterday's bacon. We ate that and sipped tea from the thermos while our minds caught up. Outside the cabin, the forest was still dark and cold, the big circular thermometer on Burian's porch reading 22°F.

I wanted to ski first, using Jan's boots which were a full size smaller than mine. My slightly swollen ankle was wrapped in a bandage, but I had to remove it before Jan's boots would fit at all. My toes were pinched even in light socks but I recalled that hockey legend Gordie Howe had reportedly skated his entire career in too-small skates. He claimed it kept him on his toes, so perhaps this would keep me hopping as well.

Maybe the dogs would have picked up some hop too, after a day's rest and more food. We'd have to see.

Before we left the cabin I began splitting a few sticks of wood to leave kindling for the next person, then realized that the noise couldn't have been appreciated. The axe-swinging had felt good at any rate, forcing me to take deep breaths of the crisp air and getting my circulation flowing.

Together we dragged the toboggan to the dog lot and stretched out the harnesses on the trail. Flander was loose; he'd slipped his collar sometime during the night and gone to sleep next to Rafferty. He could shed his collar so easily that his neck must have been bigger than his head. I grabbed the loose dog after pretending to be fussing over Rafferty, arousing his jealousy. But when I went back for Rafferty and unclipped him, he jerked from my grasp and bolted for the trees. He hid there until Jan coaxed him out. Tuk's chain was a tangle of knots, the swivel frozen, and it was only luck that he hadn't broken loose last night too. If he had, no doubt he'd have started a fight with Mrs. Burian's retired sled dogs.

Finally we had them all in harness and quiet. I put on the skis and asked Jan if she was ready.

"Yes. And freezing," she said. "Let's get going."

I led the parade to the slough behind Stewart Island and headed north along the main snowmobile trail.

Mrs. Burian had told us the trail should be alright although no one would be using it much this late in the season. We might be the last dog team travellers before spring break-up. Rudy said we should be in Dawson in two and a half days; I figured four easy days would probably be happier for all involved. Tonight we would aim for a trapper's cabin roughly a quarter of the distance to Dawson. I'd been to his cabin the previous summer, reaching it by canoe. The cabin was small and he might not be there but at least we could make camp in his yard.

As the slough opened out to the flat, white, mile-wide expanse of frozen river, I noticed the first yellow celebration of sunrise gathering in the east. Jan was having her problems behind me: Casey's old leather traces had worn through at a buckle, and a cord on Rafferty's had un-knotted itself as well. I skied ahead half a mile and back to keep my toes and fingers from getting cold. The birch skis were noticeably lighter for their weeks of springtime use and had no camber left at all. The edges were completely rounded, the bases shaggy and deeply grooved. The toboggan base was even worse. Of the seven planks comprising the run-ning surface, one was broken, one was cracked and two were worn right through at the curl. It was going to be a toss-up which would collapse first, the skis or toboggan. What we'd do when the toboggan gave out I didn't know but Danny had been right: "Maybe you're gonna have no toboggan left when you get to Stewart." Now, with the deep snow behind us, we really needed a light sleigh with metal-clad runners. There would be considerable friction on our ragged toboggan now, especially late in the day.

Jan and the dogs were mobile once more and we started again, fol-lowing the wide, well-packed snowmobile track. In places sand showed through the snow and ice; it was the only way to know when we were over sandbars and not water. A small side trail branched off, heading into the forest of an island, perhaps one of the Burian family's trapping loops.

The awesome feeling of isolation we'd known even on the Stewart River trail was not as intense here; the snow bore tracks from the passage of innumerable machines and dogs. We passed candy bar wrappers and oil cans lying on the ice waiting for spring break-up to flush away the garbage.

Rounding one island, the crust over an acre of ice abruptly settled a fraction of an inch, making a deep WOOOMP noise. The leader, Iskoot, his hair on end, turned back and crawled underneath Casey, causing another jumble and delay. We sorted them out and lifted Iskoot around back on his feet but more crust spontaneously settled, triggering another section and another so that WOOMP sounds rolled across the river flats like the pounding of a giant bass drum.

"Shit. This is too freaky for me too," Jan said. "No wonder Iskoot is afraid. Is this at all safe?"

I assured her that this was common on lakes and rivers. Freaking scary, but the ice might still be a few feet thick. It was simply settling and shifting as the water level changed below it. We peered into a nearby crack to verify over five feet of ice depth.

Iskoot was too unnerved to lead so Casey the Wonder Dog was pressed into service, and the crew continued under a barrage of threats and waved ski poles.

By early afternoon the sun was burning down fiercely on our little party, all uncomfortably hot in the 50-degree glare. We coaxed the dogs to wade through shallow puddles on the melting trail, and against the cliffs steered them around rock slides and mini avalanches. Where rock debris had fallen onto the river, melt holes marked where dark stones had absorbed the sun's heat and disappeared into the ice.

The dogs were doing their share of absorbing heat too, their tongues dripping and tempers short. None of them was pulling well; the toboggan speed was now only at a person's walking pace. Jan was doing as much as could be hoped, alternating verbal and physical encouragement. I was reminded of the qualifications to be a musher, according to bar lore: 'You have to have long legs and like to beat dogs.' The long legs presumably were for running behind or in front of the team.

"Sometimes I feel terrible hitting the dogs," Jan confessed. "But sometimes it feels good, I'm so frustrated. We know they are faking it a lot."

"Yeah, don't I know it," I commiserated. "Horse drivers use whips, and electric prods are used to move stubborn cattle. No doubt people have been frustrated by animals since the first ones were domesticated. Maybe if you had a team of dogs for years, raised and trained from pups, you could cull the bad ones and get a hard-working team. That seems to be what Cowboy and other mushers are doing. It is frustrating and down-right embarrassing having these dogs at times."

"At times. How about *all* the time?"

With three miles to go and no one enjoying themselves, we ran into a mushy section which developed into a slushy section that led into a broad, snow-covered, four-inch-deep puddle. There was no easy way around so we splashed through, soaking ourselves up to the knees and dragging the reluctant dogs by their collars. An hour later, still a mile from the cabin, a lone skidoo approached us from the north. It was the trapper, Brian McDonald, out hunting for spring bear.

Brian invited us to his cabin and looked rather contemptuously at the team. "I guess I'll have time to light a fire and boil some coffee by the time you get there with that scruffy outfit. They don't look very fast."

Perhaps it was the smell of another cabin or the prospect of a rest ahead, but the dogs perked right up and we managed to arrive and have them chained up well before the coffee was ready.

Waiting, mug in hand, Jan was delighted to hear Brian say about his stove, "Some airtights ain't worth a shit. Maybe I should shoot it again."

He let her know he was kidding, he really hadn't shot his stove – yet. But if a mouse were standing on it, "If they come out in the open, they are fair game!"

Without much encouragement, he soon had us outside blasting away at targets and empty oil cans, whooping it up in Wild West fashion. Off to the side, the dogs were cringing and nervously burrowing into the snow.

After a big mid-afternoon meal of moose meat and rice – "That's the only thing on the menu here," Brian announced proudly – we talked into the evening. Then we had another big feed of moose but with some of our food to accompany it, plus bread Cybil had baked and tucked in as an extra treat.

I tried to interview Brian, as I had ambitions of selling recordings to CBC Radio, but only captured half a cassette of giggled silliness. Why be serious? Life is too short. On that note, we decided to 'hit the sack' as it was midnight, with the alarm set for six.

Jan and I stretched out in the kitchen on the plank floor, happy to have a roof over our heads and a warm cabin around us. Brian said he wouldn't shoot any mice without warning us first to keep our heads down, and blew out the lamp. "Well, that's only a *maybe*," he added. "No guarantees at this hotel."

"Is this what roadhouses were like?" Jan whispered to me. "Kinda fun."

CHAPTER 22

EARLY TO RISE, EARLY TO STOP

Brian was up before the alarm and relighting the stove when the dogs started barking. In a moment, we too could hear the distant whine of approaching snowmobiles.

So much for coffee in bed, I thought and got dressed as well.

Soon the dogs' noise was drowned out by a roar, and then all was quiet. The door opened – Robin and Ivan Burian burst in, pulling off mitts and brushing snow from their pant legs.

"We're going to town," they announced to Brian. "Are you coming?"

He hesitated only a moment. Then he said to us, "Make yourselves at home. Fix some breakfast. There's coffee in that can and fry some moose if you want… Now where's my mitt?"

It was still quite dark in the little cabin and we all searched for Brian's other mitt without success. He had to settle for a well worn mismatch from an old pair. Apologizing for running off on us, he did just that, jumped onto his steed and gunned the machine after his friends.

In a minute, the world was still and quiet again, the only sound from the crackling kindling in the cookstove. In a few hours they'd be in Dawson; at the same time we would be only a few miles down the trail.

This trip is beginning to drag, I said to myself, and realized Jan was thinking the same thing. We packed up while waiting for the coffee water to boil.

"I'll ski first," Jan offered.

The dogs, with Iskoot leading again, kept up to Jan for a half hour before starting to lose interest. The trail was rough, following the east cliffs and often on a shelf of shore ice. Once in a while it swung out onto the wild jagged ice of mid-channel to avoid open water. The toboggan dumped many times on the uneven track but I had no trouble lifting it back upright. It was either getting much lighter or I was stronger.

There is a beauty, a fascination, and a danger out there on the frozen Yukon. Ice-snow diamonds mesmerize the eye, magic crystals reflecting and refracting the sun's glare, burning the unshielded cornea. Dunes of blown snow blanket the surface in deceptive thicknesses – sometimes paper thin, often past your ankle.

From my position behind the toboggan, I imagined the dogs as they should be: fur rippling as their bodies bob and roll with each pulling step; an easy fluid motion with the back legs slightly splayed, tail down, heads nodding with a dancer's rhythm. This band of gypsy mongrels had no style: some tails high and even wagging, lines slack, most not leaning, just keeping up. Flander was hopeless. Only Mitti had even, clean movement. The others were just plodders – hulking brutes who needed training beyond our capabilities. The dog fighting had been unsettling: a small problem grows, dissension spreads; non-cooperation seems to increase exponentially.

Should have been stricter from the start, I thought, and should have insisted Jan was too. However, this team was still functioning, and were all we had. We'd get there even though it wasn't much fun and not at all fast.

When I knelt beside Tuk to adjust his harness, he nudged my armpit with his snout, trying to lift my arm. This sled dog, 100 pounds of bone and muscle and fur and teeth, who liked nothing so much as the chance to rip another dog apart, could still be as coy at pawing, playing and licking as the silliest little house pet. He clearly wanted a few pats under his scarred chin, perhaps a tickle behind his ripped ear. Over this trip, we'd learned a bit about judging their energy levels and actual effort. Unfortunately, they'd been ill-served by our lack of experience and knowledge.

Back in motion, I had time to think of the poster dog team image: mask-like faces, powerful chests, proud curled tails. Now I was getting the reverse view: a long line of doggie behinds wiggling like high-heeled ladies' bottoms, tails up to expose six brown eyes. Then one winked! Within seconds the toboggan was pulled into a warm cloud of fishy-putrid stench, and mercifully on through, back into cold, fresh air. Apparently their bowels would take time adjusting to the new dog food. It would be a 'whiffy' day.

Her boots soaked from skiing into an overflow puddle and sporting her baby-blue pyjama suit rolled down to the waist, Jan was waiting, always way ahead, outdistancing us even on the straight, flat sections. She'd developed a relaxed stride, certainly not classical, yet controlled and assured. We'd come a long way in more than just distance, I was realizing. I had to laugh. I just felt happy.

"Hey, speed queen!" I yelled to her. "Time out. Lunch! It's too hot. TOO HOT! LUNCH!"

She skated back and we dug out the makings of a meal. We were stopped adjacent to a small island with smaller poplars.

"How far do you reckon we've come this morning?" she asked.

"Maybe 12 miles. Maybe 15 at most."

Jan had unpacked the tarp to sit on and we trampled a path to the island to make ourselves a comfortable picnic spot. The dogs were sprawled on the track, still in their harnesses but soon asleep.

"Sitting sure beats going anywhere," Jan said finally.

"I'll get your book," I agreed and brought back the sleeping bags from the toboggan as well. "Might as well be comfortable. I vote we camp right here."

"Yes, let's just stay here. I'm enjoying being right here where I don't have to think about my Whitehorse life. We'll get there soon enough, without me worrying. I feel perfect in this moment, right where I am."

CHAPTER 23

END OF THE TOBOGGAN

An hour after dawn we were underway, about a mile out from where we'd camped, when Jan stopped and pointed ahead with a ski pole. Three dark dots were weaving across the snow in the distance, moving rapidly in our direction. With the toboggan stopped, I could now hear the whining engines ever increasing in volume. It was Robin, Ivan and Brian, coming back from Dawson.

They pulled around us and shared tea from our thermos. Brian assured us he'd alerted Alan Nordling and John Tapsell in Dawson that we were safe and coming. Slowly. "I told him you might be a while," he added and nodded at the dogs.

Robin asked what we were planning to do when the toboggan fell apart.

"Try to use the skis to make runners, or just leave everything and walk into Dawson, are the only ideas I've got," I said. "Guess we'll figure it out when, if, we need to."

Thanking us for tea, the three made ready to drive away when Brian remembered, "If you make it to town for Saturday night, there's a dance on. Today is Friday."

And they were off, zooming wherever they pleased on the morning crust, making hardly any impression on the frozen expanse.

We mushed on, Jan still on skis. I was alternating standing on the tail and running behind to keep warm. The dogs were following her well, along the winding trail out to the mid-river where the jamming, freezing, thawing, refreezing, bucking, thrusting iceflows had disoriented the surface. Massive blocks of ice lay in folds across our route. The trail wound around, over, between, over, through – to help negotiate the corners, I balanced the toboggan on a knife edge and pumped with my free leg. Even so it was taking a severe beating as we bounced over the ice jumble.

"Hold on, fella," I said to the toboggan. "We're almost there."

Jan was waiting for us, but didn't race ahead when we caught up. Instead she lifted one foot to show me half a ski. It had almost worn through under the heel before it snapped. "Any chance of a warranty on these?" she called.

"It began to feel like a piece of spaghetti," she explained, "so I knew it would break soon."

"So much for skiing."

"Yep, so much for skiing. Just when I was getting pretty good at it."

"You were. And so much for making runners to put under the toboggan," I added. "Guess we'll think of something when we need to."

"Necessity is the mother of invention, right?"

"And if we invented the necessity, does that make us grandparents of invention?"

"I guess. Or idiots."

We took turns running ahead of the dogs. We'd only had one switch, though, before we neared a trapper's cabin and homestead at Galena Creek. It was Roger Mendelsohn's place and his Siberian sled dogs were kicking up enough racket to welcome two hundred visitors. Our dogs pulled noticeably faster when they heard the greetings. We were just chaining them to trees near the rampway up the bank when Roger and his three-year-old son, Mark, appeared.

He immediately invited us in, asking if we'd had lunch yet.

"Well, we had a snack just a while back," I said, but happily he wasn't deterred by this.

"How about a few eggs for lunch? Fresh eggs laid this morning? And coffee!"

The offer was inspired. Our last egg meal was the powdered-egg-frisbee on Scroggie Creek we couldn't finish. Anything would beat that.

'A few eggs' turned out to be a heaping plateful each of scrambled eggs. Jan and I wolfed them down, taking turns to answer questions and describe our trip. Over coffee, Roger explained how the processes of hen raising, goat ranching, trapping, championship dog breeding, market gardening, raising two children and building a splendid log house had kept him and his wife Donna – who was in Dawson with baby Anne – very busy.

The house's roof was composed of thin peeled poles, over 300 in all, overlaid with poly plastic and fibreglass insulation batting, then a foot of moss, and finally sheets of tin. Rain could run off the metal into gutters which filled rain barrels for irrigation.

The interior of the log walls was insulated and panelled, while the outside was banked high with earth. Roger and Donna were taking no chances of being cold.

"Don't the goats attract bears?" I asked.

"No problem at all there," Roger said and smiled. "I like bear. Bears fit nicely in quart sealer jars. I prefer bear to any other game meat."

When a bear showed up last year on the hillside above the farm, the dogs barked up a storm. It was getting too dark for a good shot, Roger told us, so he aimed high to scare it off. His shot, however, was low, killing the bear instantly. The body rolled down the hill, coming to rest against one of the dog houses. That dog, who'd barked so fiercely moments before, now was trapped, terrified, in his house, the door completely blocked by bear fur.

"We couldn't get that dog to come out, even the next day," Roger laughed. "He wouldn't come out until I shovelled away all the blood, too. I guess he could still smell that bear."

Roger gave us a quart mason jar of bear meat for our supper on the trail. I'd never tasted bear before so was really looking forward to the treat.

Slippery Flander was loose again and all Roger's dogs were alarmed, so we decided to take our leave before any incident spoiled the visit. Roger walked us back down to the river and stared in amazement at the flimsy toboggan relic.

"Could I lend you my dog sleigh?" he asked gently. "That one might not make it much further."

With little hesitation we accepted his generous offer and were soon transferring our gear into a beautiful, handcrafted 10-foot-long hardwood sleigh. It stood tall on runners clad in smooth polished metal. The entire basket of the sleigh was made of hardwood slats, sanded and varnished, pegged and tied together with raw moosehide strips, yet it weighed no more than our shorter toboggan. Our outfit – duffles and boxes, snowshoes and dogfood sacks – was dwarfed on the big sleigh.

Yet more importantly there was almost zero friction with those metal runners – you could easily push the loaded sleigh with one hand.

We rolled the old toboggan on its side and took a picture to show the Pelly farmers. There were only two intact planks left out of seven. The others were broken or worn away completely at the curl. We wouldn't have been able to coax too many more miles from it, likely not as far as Dawson. What a blessing to meet Roger.

With our flashy sleigh and bottle of bear meat, we left Roger to make "a few more miles so tomorrow will be easier."

"Just leave the sleigh and empty jar at my mother's house in Dawson," he called and we waved in acknowledgement.

The dogs seemed to appreciate the smoother load but the sleigh was tricky to control, slipping sideways off the trail on slanted places, though it was much easier to turn at corners. When it left the track and buried itself in the soft snow, either Jan or I would casually lift the hundreds of pounds back onto the trail and mush on. We were both unquestionably stronger for our journey.

By late afternoon we had covered perhaps eight miles from Roger's and were eyeing various campsites when a helicopter flew up the valley and landed on the far side, behind an island. Five minutes later, its errand apparently done, it rose over the trees, spun around and jetted back to town. The chopper would be there in minutes; we still had 20 long miles to go. It seemed so futile, all this effort.

"Let's go to that next chain of islands," I suggested to Jan who was looking tired.

"Okay," she said, "but let's stop soon."

I had been mushing so I let her ride instead, and ran off ahead,

Mark Mendelsohn poses beside our worn-out toboggan. It clearly could not have taken us much farther over the ice and crusty snow.

calling for Iskoot to follow. Soon we were halfway across the clear area and then only 200 yards from the islands.

"We'll be there soon," I yelled over my shoulder, reaching for my pocket watch.

Then I went through the ice.

"Holyshit. Sonofabitch," I muttered slowly, standing calf-deep in water. My heart was pounding. My body was shaking from the surge of adrenalin. I took a deep breath, and then another.

Then I slowly lifted one leg out onto the trail behind me. A large plate of ice and snow broke off and floated against my legs. Cautiously I tested the next section and it flexed but held, barely.

I stepped fully up onto the trail and walked back to the team, my wet pants slapping against each other. I had only fallen through into water flowing over another layer of ice – overflow – but I was scared.

"We can't go that way. We'll have to find a way around," I said to Jan, still shaking.

I took a ski pole to test the ice and began probing for good trail. This morning's trio of snowmobile tracks clearly led across the hole I'd just made but their speed had made the difference.

Jan was moving up the dogs a healthy distance behind me, watching closely as I tested and rejected a few places. We were progressing in a wide semi-circle, turned away from the islands we'd hoped to camp on. As the adrenalin wore off I was getting quite tired now, too, and the dogs began acting up and refused to follow. Large grey patches in the river's snow and ice cover flanked us on either side, ominous warnings of flowing water underneath. Here we were, only fifty yards from the apparently safe main trail, picking our way through a maze of rotten ice, not knowing whether there was a solution to this labyrinth.

I went back to help Jan persuade the dogs through a slushy section and could see the frustration in her eyes. "Soon… Soon," was all I could offer.

With heart in mouth, ski pole in hand – and, someone might add, 'a good luck horseshoe up my ass' – I tiptoed over toward a protruding gravel bar. Downstream 50 yards was open, flowing, black water. We could go no further that way. I poked at the snow. It was solid here. I moved forward, poked again. Here it wasn't. I eased back and prodded some more parallel to the bar, but it was all the same punky crust.

So the question was: how deep is the overflowing water, assuming there is an underlayer of ice? I probed with the ski pole and found an area where the water was only ankle deep. I splashed across to stand in the knee-deep snow beside a log lying on the gravel. It looked so incongruous there in the middle of a sea of snow to have one log, but it was a most welcome marker of safe ground.

I splashed back to where Iskoot and the others were rebelling, and led them through the water until they were on the bar and foundering in the deeper snow. Jan was pushing on the sleigh while I pulled it almost to the log, and finally we were all on firm footing. Then we stomped a trail across the bar, found better ice below it, and could regain the snow-mobile trail just as it reached the first island.

This wasn't a very good site. It didn't matter if the snow was too deep everywhere, if there were spruce needles in all the snow we intended to melt for drinking water, if there were thorny rosebushes grabbing at us constantly. We didn't complain about carrying all the food and gear around and up an impossibly steep bank, or about the lack of small dead wood. We were glad to be there. With a sip of tea from the thermos, I perked up a little and found the energy to saw up a green tree for a reflector fire so we could have enough radiant heat to comfortably dry our footwear.

The bear meat was rich and tasty, with two packages of macaroni dinner as side orders. The little we didn't finish was left on the plates for breakfast but covered over so the whiskey jacks wouldn't help themselves. The dogs finished off their bag of dogfood, with Iskoot getting the extra crumbs for all his tense leadership. "Just one more day," I told him as he yawned, "and you'll get a ride all the way home to Three-Quarter Jon."

He rested his head on his paws and looked at me with an old dog's eyes.

Jan had the sleeping bags laid out near the fire and was turning socks over as they steam-dried on a rope. Her cracked, scorch-scarred ski boots were wet still and the moccasins and toe rubbers were also.

"I wonder sometimes what it's like to have dry feet all day. And warm ones, too," she said, staring into the flames and rubbing her toes. The flames reflected in her eyes and off her snow-tanned cheeks, her face so much thinner from the twenty days on the trail. I'd never seen a woman look finer.

As Jan fell asleep, I stayed up frying a half-dozen bannocks for us to eat cold in the morning and as lunch. I raked a bed of cherry-red coals out from the fire for the cast frying pan to sit on. To the lard I added a dollop of bear grease I'd saved from Roger's jar of meat. For what seemed like a blissful eternity, I watched the fat buggers sizzling until golden brown on each side. Not quite cosmic, I thought, tasting one, but they *are* getting better.

Finally I tried to memorize every detail of the fire, every sparkle, the placement of each log, the flames. Then I closed my eyes and held that last campfire of our trip firmly in my mind as I slept.

CHAPTER 24

RUNNING, RUNNING TO DAWSON

Once more, before dawn, we were awake and packing. Yet everything seemed just a bit different because this was our last time.

There was a solid crust on the trail; yesterday had been very warm before last night's deep frost. Without difficulty, we were able to cover five miles in the first hour. Jan and I took turns running ahead, switching as soon as one got winded. By the time the sun was high we were already stripped down to shirtsleeves and still too hot. The six dogs raced along with the smooth sleigh presenting almost no resistance. I had to hold them back to guard Jan's heels.

"Maybe we're going to make it after all," I marvelled as the islands flashed by.

Near Bell Creek we could hear a dog team barking but we didn't stop in to visit – we wanted to make time, we wanted to *make it*.

Jan was running in front when the trail threaded between two pools of water about 20 feet apart. The water appeared clear and shallow. I could see the gravel bottom as she ran onto the bridge of ice and snow.

It collapsed under her.

For a moment she stood up to her thighs in the icy water, and then calmly climbed out. I started to unpack a pair of pants for her to change into, but she stopped me.

"I'll just get wet again," she said and ran off again, making a wide sweep around the pools and back onto the trail.

When we again caught up to her, she was standing beside the trail waiting to trade places. "That's a helluva way to wake up," she laughed.

My felt boot liners were soggy. They had never really dried out over the fire and a fresh soaker made them heavier. Pac boots were never made to run in but they were all I had except frozen moccasins and toe-less ski boots, so I ran, ignoring the weight. Hell, I thought, they don't weigh nearly as much wet as they did with snowshoes attached.

The effort behind us on the trip was paying off now: we were almost effortlessly jogging away the miles, with muscles we'd never had before.

I looked back after running through a slushy spot beside another puddle. As the sleigh started to slide sideways towards the water, Jan hopped off the back and ran in the water, steering and pushing to keep the load upright and on the track. With the sleigh safely past, she scrambled aboard as if this was simply routine. Indeed, mushing seemed natural for this ex-pat from the Edgewater Tavern.

Soon we were watching ore trucks hugging the hilltop curves of the Top-of-the-World Highway and could see the Moosehide Slide and Midnight Dome of Dawson City in the distance. We ate lunch perched on a great log beside the trail. It was sunny and would be very hot later.

"What are you thinking about?" I asked.

"Truck payment. Rent."

"Sounds like you are pretty sure we're going to make it to Dawson."

With Dawson City in sight, we can *almost* relax. There is, however, still the matter of crossing the mouth of the Klondike River.

"Yep. Had some doubts a few times, I'll admit," she said, eating some snow.

Just out of Dawson, we posed for photographs with the town in the background.

"Need them to prove we were here," I said. "When you are sixty years old, your grandkids won't believe half of what we've been through, I'll bet."

"I'm not sure I believe it," she said and smiled.

We jogged past Sunnydale Farm and came upon the mother of all ice jumbles before the mouth of the Klondike River. Our route snaked through a bizarre random arrangement of massive ice blocks, each 10-feet cubed or larger, jammed into rows and clusters like pillars and dwellings of an ancient temple city.

If we'd encountered anything like this on the Yukon River below Selkirk, we'd never have gotten through, I thought while steering the sleigh along the narrow alleyway between blocks.

Our last obstacle was the mouth of the Klondike itself where there was a 30-yard-wide ice bridge across the otherwise wildly-flowing shallow river. Here, the traffic of snowmachines travelling across the river-mouth throughout the winter had compacted the snow and pounded the frost deeper than surrounding areas. The result was thicker ice, frozen right to the river bottom.

"At least that's the theory," I told Jan.

"You don't sound totally convinced."

At that moment, as if to reassure us, a snowmobile raced across and hurried past us up the Yukon.

We walked the dogs and sleigh across, then chained them to bushes and rusted mining-machinery relics that protruded from the Front Street dike. We were finally in Dawson City. I felt like crying. Jan wore the biggest grin, proclaiming her triumph and relief.

"We're here!" I wanted to scream but couldn't find my voice. We walked together slowly to Alan Nordling's and found him and John Tapsell making lunch. They'd heard from Brian McDonald and were expecting us today.

"Looks like you two could use a bath," Alan said. "There are towels in the bathroom and you can stay in the second bedroom. But I guess we'd better fetch your dogs first. John was just telling me how much he missed his two. How'd they make out?"

"Yeah," John added, "we've been figuring out that nobody has come through with dogs in the winter from Selkirk to Dawson in maybe twenty, even thirty years. What took you so long?"

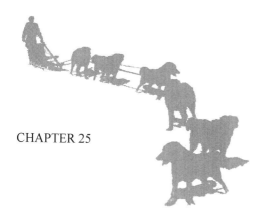

CHAPTER 25

CONTINUING THE QUEST

W aking up in a bed felt strange. The house was toasty warm with its central heating blasting away throughout the night. I looked at my watch and noted it was only six-thirty; my trail habits were still turned on.

I tip-toed around the house, restless and missing having a fire to light or somewhere to rush off toward. The 20-odd days in the wilderness had been a lifetime in a parallel world, one without the television, phone, electric frying pan, stereo, couches, light bulbs – and all the other objects here in the livingroom. Impulsively I weighed myself on the bathroom scales and was shocked to be only 129 pounds; I'd shed 16 pounds. Likely Jan had lost even more weight – she'd been turning heads as we'd transferred gear from riverside to this house.

A glance in the mirror revealed an unfamiliar body: an ectomorphic skeleton clad only in muscle and sinew, not an ounce of fat anywhere in sight. My stomach was concave, my thighs rock hard. The skin on my face, neck, hands and forearms was leathery brown; elsewhere I was pasty pale.

John Tapsell interrupted my musing with news. There was an

immediate job opening at the elementary school for a night-shift janitor; the last custodian had quit, citing medical reasons. "He kept muttering about 'spray buff madness'," John said, "but you won't have to worry because you're already crazy."

Sure, I could do that for a while, I knew. Letting the world pop opportunities in front of me just seemed natural at this point in my life.

Casey was barking from the empty lot across the road where the dogs were tied, so I put on a jacket and boots and went out to quiet him.

Whatever was bothering him must have moved on because he'd settled down before I got to the street. When he spotted me, he whined and jumped about frantically as was his habit. When I didn't immediately cross, he stopped, lay again in the trampled snow and whimpered morosely. Iskoot answered with a puppy's thin wail. Tuk offered a few gravelly comments, tentatively howled, then looked about hesitantly. Mitti was silent. I waited, but the lusty wolf-pack howling of our trip never materialized. Somehow they, too, knew this adventure was over. The smells and heat of Northern spring were about us, winter travel dissipating from their thoughts. They would probably forget how they'd come to Dawson even before their thick fur had begun to shed.

Jan would be off today, hitching a ride to Pelly, taking Tuk, Mitti and Iskoot back to their Whitehorse owners.

Before she left, we walked to Front Street in the 65°F warmth, not really saying much about the trip. Looking out over the Klondike River mouth, we realized the ice bridge we'd crossed yesterday had washed away. Some angels must have been watching over us. "Or those UFOs," Jan offered.

As we sat on the gravel bank, a long list of should-have's came to mind, hard to ignore. "For my next trips, I'll know a lot better," I offered, "about a lot of things… Jan, you were amazing out there. Really amazing. That was the most gruelling trip I've ever been on. Most guys would have given up. I sure hope this trip doesn't put you off camping altogether."

"Oh no. Some parts of it were good, and I'm glad I did it," she said, flipping pebbles onto the muddy shoreline below us. "I sure proved some things to myself. I feel kinda proud. I just need to sort out my life right now," she added. "You know, a summer job, rent money. That stuff. But I want to do more, see more, still, for sure… Thanks for taking me along, Bruce."

"Hey, it was your idea, remember? You asked," I said. "I figure you gotta try if you want to learn. Just like Abby told us at Fort Selkirk: she helped and watched the old people. Learning by doing. Whether it is travelling with dogs, or working in an art auction house… Thanks for being my partner."

Then Jan walked away, leaving me sitting alone on the bank. Looking out across the river, I realized the voices of others were no longer badgering away inside my head. Their anxieties, worries and pressures had faded away. Instead I was beginning to listen to my heart.

My personal quest seemed entwined with the lives of the territory's pioneers: the Indians and early white sourdoughs, the trappers and mail team wranglers. My great-grandfather had been a '98 stampeder, a seasoned prospector from the Kamloops area who had rushed to the Klondike with forty thousand others. Theirs was a year-long ordeal of packing supplies over the Chilkoot Pass, wintering at Lindeman Lake, whipsawing logs into planks to build boats, and paddling down the Yukon River. For most of them, their hopes and dreams were shattered when they reached Dawson to discover all the best ground had been claimed and there would be no quick wealth. Yet they were all richer in experience, the quest for fortune leaving an indelible mark on their characters.

The sun was baking hot and the snow around me melting fast – you could almost see the crust evaporating while rivulets trickled down everywhere along the bank. Out on the Yukon River, still frozen clear across, the ice surface was flexing and compressing, imperceptibly from where I sat, but within two weeks, the strain of flooding melt water would be released in a night of crashing ice pans and rumbling flows. Spring break-up was queued up for its place in the river's cycle.

EPILOGUE

J anet Prenty didn't move to Manhattan or London, and never pursued working for an art auction house. Instead she married a trapper and raised a family living on a trapline, relying on dogs, skis and snowmobiles for winter transportation. She has two grown daughters and three grandchildren, and cross-country skis on the Canadian Olympic team's training trails near Whitehorse.

My night-shift custodian job lasted only a week. While I worked, Casey the Wonder Dog howled into the wee hours every night, prompting a delegation of irate neighbours to orchestrate my pink slip. Fortunately I soon secured a high-wage gig surveying for a Dempster Highway construction outfit. At their trailer camp, Casey befriended the cooks who fed him so well he slept quite contentedly. That job earned me enough money to embark on canoe trips, which flowed into autumn hunts, and then winter treks. A few years later I assembled two ragtag dog teams, this time to spend a whole winter living six miles downstream from Fort Selkirk and travelling across the snowy landscape. My partner was Marsha McGillis, who later became my wife. That experience is chronicled in *Nine Dog Winter [Victoria, BC: Agio Publishing House, 2008]*.

Some of my bush learning also found its way into *The Lost Whole Moose Catalogue: A Yukon Way of Knowledge [Whitehorse, YT: Rock & Roll Moose Meat Collective, 1979]*.

2

COST-PLUS

Each bush job was a new adventure: people to meet, remote places to experience, situations to learn from. Some were downright crazy.

COST-PLUS

"*Cost-plus* means they pay for everything and then pay me five percent more for my salary," Tom explained, pulling his *Mayo Helicopters* baseball cap down tightly over his short cropped hair while his other hand chucked tins into the shopping cart. A pipe, which he rarely lit but affected to look older than his twenty years, bobbed up and down as he spoke. "It's probably a tax write-off for them anyways. Oil companies have lots of money."

"So we eat smoked oysters? And T-bones?" The groceries were going to cost a pretty penny. Food was never cheap in Whitehorse.

"Caviar, too, if they've got any in this store," he went on, and then spied the candy section. "Candy. Oh yes. *Lots* of candy!" He began grabbing bags of bonbons and cases of chocolate bars. So much for appearing mature.

The liquor aisle was the same sideshow. Johnny Walker Scotch, bottles of vodka, rye, imported wines for supper. "We *gotta* have Kahlúa in our coffee for breakfast," he said, and a few cases of beer "for after a hard day's work!"

The *work*, this plum-of-a-contract Tom had somehow managed to score, was an oil-lease clean-up on the Eagle Plains north-east of Dawson City, not far from where the new Dempster Highway would go. Old oil drilling sites last used in the early 1950s suddenly had to have the garbage picked up. No one seemed to know exactly why this belated housekeeping was needed 25 years later, but windfall jobs weren't to be questioned closely, in the tradition of a gift horse or a free round for the house. If *they* wanted to blow their money, I didn't mind eating oysters. On this project I was hired as labourer and cook. Tom was the *boss*, and Bob would be the only other labourer, so I'd be cooking for only four including the helicopter pilot. There was enough alcohol in the cart for a regiment and we were only going for a week to ten days.

"Here, you pay for the booze. I'm not old enough," he said, passing me three $50 bills. "Be sure to get the receipt, eh?"

Departure Morning

Six o'clock, after three hours sleep, the stupid little alarm clock was hopping about the table, waking the dead, and me-who-wished-he-was-dead. I was suffering from what you might call your standard hangover but about twenty times more intense. Tom, arriving twenty minutes later, after I'd just fallen back to sleep, somehow managed to coax me to drink some tomato juice and stumble out into his rented truck. "We'll be late. We'll be late," he said and roared away like the Mad Hatter on wheels. I rested my forehead on the dashboard and tried to sleep. That didn't help.

"Fug you!! Leemealone, fug you guys. Sumabitch! Fug…" was all we could get Bob to say. He was still fully drunk and raring to fight although he was also eighty or ninety percent asleep. His black hair was drenched in sweat and his eyes held that glazed look that meant he won't remember any of this.

We argued with him – more like *at* him – for a few minutes but ducked out when he took a wild swing at Tom. If he had been smaller we might have dragged him along, but Bob outweighed both of us.

On the plus side it looked like I'd be cooking for only three. On the minus side, I'd be doing all the labourer work, whatever that was going to be. Tom was disappointed, mostly because Bob was a status Indian, and that meant, in Tom's misinterpretation of the law, that Tom could have killed any wildlife we encountered. Having no Bob was surely a plus side development for the birds and caribou.

Cessna 180

Imagine an old Volkswagen beetle with wings, and no muffler. Now imagine it a whole lot louder and bouncing and dropping all over the sky. My eyes were burning and swollen, my stomach ready to bail out and I hoped we would crash soon so I could get some sleep. Planes are not a good place for a morning-after.

"If you get sick in my plane you can clean it up!" yelled the pilot as he turned to hand me a small paper bag.

"Thanks!" I yelled back.

"What?!"

"Never mind!"

"What?!" he asked again. He pointed at the bag and yelled, "Barf in here! Throw up! Sick!" and turned back to look at the bleak sky ahead.

I peered into the bag and wondered what he would do with it if I did get sick in it. Throw it out the window? Drop it on a caribou? Splat! Yech.

Two hours later, Tom turned around from his seat beside the pilot, his baseball cap pulled low. "Ogilvies!" he shouted, breathing last night's Scotch all over the cabin and gesturing out the port window. "This is the Tombstone Range."

My heart leapt. Jagged, soaring spires of snow-capped rock crowded a narrow canyon with the thread of a river in its depths. The white mountains were a fortress of turrets, powerful, awesome and bleak, yet brilliant in the morning sun's soft light.

The Cessna tipped and slid sideways down into that canyon and we flew on, racing our shadow across the dazzling mountain faces. Surely these were Middle Earth's Misty Mountains, I thought, and looked for orks.

Ninety minutes later we were buzzing low over the Eagle Plains; flat, forested with miniature black trees and meadowed in muskeg.

"Is that it?" The pilot was pointing at a bare patch just ahead.

Tom had a topographical map open on his lap but he wasn't paying much attention to it. He seemed nervous. "No… No," he yelled, "it's over there more!"

How they were navigating at all was a mystery to me, as there were no significant landmarks. It was pancake-flat in all directions with only the occasional low pimple mound. The marshy wetlands were infinitely random inkblots. Tom had been out here once before, though, and perhaps he knew his way around. But if he did, why did he sound so nervous?

The wheels were bouncing on a gravel runway a few minutes later and we taxied to a stop beside a dozen fuel barrels. After getting out, we rolled one over to the Cessna and used a hand-pump to fill the tanks. The 45-gallon drum was stenciled *Forestry*. "They won't miss it," said the pilot. Then we unloaded all our food and booze and backpacks.

"This is it?" I asked Tom. There were no buildings.

"No, this is where we meet the chopper," he explained. "There's a Hughes 500 helicopter coming from Norman Wells in the N.W.T. I chartered it for the week to move the garbage. He should be here soon."

We stood there shivering in the September breeze as the Cessna revved its engine. We waved as it bounced down the crude strip and hopped into the sky. When again it was quiet, and too late, I looked at Tom. "Are you *sure* that helicopter is coming, Tom?"

"Oh yeah. I told him the map co-ordinates over the phone and he said he'd be here at eleven. Relax. Which box are the candies in?"

While he ripped food boxes apart, I glanced at my pocket watch. It was eleven-twenty. Twelve-twenty by Norman Wells time. I was pretty sure we didn't have a radio in our gear.

I dug out my parka and sat on a box of liquor, the cool air clearing my head a little.

An hour later we were relieved to hear an engine noise on the horizon – but to our dismay, it did not come our way. We were somewhere in the Eagle Plains, over two hundred miles from the nearest town. Dawson City was one very long and miserable muskeg hike away. I started making sandwiches but found it difficult to butter the bread with my fingers crossed like that.

Joe

At one-fifteen there was a deafening explosion of noise at tree-top level behind us. That, and a blinding dust storm, announced the prodigal pilot had arrived. We held our hands over our ears and squinted as the egg-shaped craft hovered near us, rocking back and forth while the grinning jockey surveyed the dirt tornado he was causing. Pick a spot, any spot, you ninny, I thought.

"Hi. I'm Joe," he drawled when he finally shut the thing off. "Best pilot in the best helicopter there is. I flew these in Viet Nam for two years. This job'll be chicken shit."

This was my first time in a helicopter and I was thrilled. The cabin of a Hughes 500 is mostly clear plexiglas. From the front seats one can see beside, above, in front, below and a fair amount behind. Joe delighted us in flying the chopper on its side and swooping down on interesting spots. With barely perceptible movements of the cyclic stick, collective lever and pedals, he'd hover, spin for a 360-degree view, then accelerate with the nose tilted down, streaking over the muskeg and stunted forest at 175 miles per hour with the jet turbine howling. I'll never bother with a roller coaster ride at an exhibition again. I've been on the best with the best.

Our first stop was Parkin Airstrip, the abandoned central supply airbase for the oil exploration companies. Situated on a low flat mound, surrounded on all sides by endless plains, this was once *home* for the drill crews. There were still a half dozen fully stocked ATCO trailers, sheets on beds, complete kitchens and dining rooms – it wasn't hard to imagine the drillers still here. The piles of skin magazines and the obscenities scrawled on the walls lent an unmistakable *I-hate-this-place* ambience.

One trailer had been visited by a bear. We weren't sure if polar bears came this far from the coast, only that this must have been one *huge* bru-in. The bear had torn a door off, ripped the hell out of many mattresses, crapped everywhere, then calmly shredded the back wall in making his exit. Why use the same door twice, eh? Make your own.

"Let's hope he's gone somewhere to hibernate," Joe suggested.

"Oh, don't worry," said Tom, "I got my elephant gun."

He had indeed brought a .460 Weatherby Magnum. There's a rifle that could also make a new trailer doorway.

In the barn-size garage were a front-end loader and a road grader, and behind the building was a huge pit, easily 50 by 50 feet and 30 feet deep.

"We'll drop the garbage in this pit," Tom said solemnly.

We must be looking at cleaning up a lot of garbage to fill that hole, I thought.

"Do we stay here?"

"No, this is another gas stop," he said as we ambled over to the fuel cache on the far side of the airstrip. Painted orange or blue or black or khaki green and stenciled with names of gas exploration companies, government branches, and air charter firms, there were perhaps three hundred 45-gallon drums.

Joe was scrambling over the rows looking for JP4, the jet fuel his chopper burns. JP4 is a 50:50 kerosene-gasoline blend, he explained as we pumped up his tanks and filled four 10-gallon drums which we placed on the back seat.

"Now where?" he asked me.

I shrugged and nodded at Tom. "He's the boss."

"A cabin," was all Tom would say, "that way."

Amazingly enough twenty minutes later we were parked beside a squat cabin built of ten-inch thick logs. Nowhere within a hundred miles was there a single tree with a diameter of more than six inches. How the cabin got there could only be explained by its foundation of three huge flattened logs which would have been used as skids for dragging it the hundreds of miles, probably by tractor train, and definitely in winter as this was muskeg country with no summer roads.

We carried the food boxes inside, discovering that the last occupant had been rather untidy. The insides were smashed and covered in bear shit. The place was a disaster. I wondered if this was the same bear. No new door but it was obviously harder to claw through log walls than an ATCO trailer.

Joe managed to bend and pry the wood-burning heater back into a usable shape and we propped the table up with pieces of shelf board. Using a piece of cardboard for a scoop we gathered up much of the excrement, putting it in a corner with all the smashed cans and shreds of bedding.

Tom lit the butane lantern and poured us each four fingers of scotch. I set up the camp stove and fished some potatoes, steaks and onions from one of the grub boxes.

Joe was watching my preparations with more than casual interest, so I finally asked him if he had a preference about how I cooked the potatoes.

He grinned wide, but said seriously, "Cook them like kidneys."

I hesitated, a bit confused, then walked into number one of Joe's two jokes. "How's that?" I asked.

"Boil the piss out of them!" he said and howled merrily as he poured another round of Scotch. "Pilots aren't supposed to drink, so this isn't happening," he grinned.

Zackallies

In the morning coffee we did indeed have the coffee liqueur. We needed it. Because, as Joe proclaimed, it is the best cure for a bad case of the *zackallies*.

"What's that?" I asked innocently.

"The zackallies are when your mouth tastes ex-zack-a-lee like your asshole!" he proclaimed smugly. For the whole time we were together, Joe never told a new joke, but he also never failed to say *cook it like kidneys* at mealtimes and diagnose *zackallies* each morning. These two jokes were as much a part of him as his goofy grin.

Tom directed us to the first site to be cleaned. The cement-filled metal pipe protruding from the centre of a cleared acre was labelled as *Socony-Mobil 1952* or some such name and year, but the area nearby bore more recent signs of a caterpillar tractor. Tom explained that tractors had come in last winter to bury the big remains but hadn't been able to dispose of the smaller stuff because it was covered in snow.

Into the helicopter's cargo net we gathered a half-ton of flattened oil drums, tin cans, drill parts and cables. It became my job to fasten the net to a large hook dangling from the chopper while Joe and Tom hovered above me. More challenging than the typhoon-force winds was the massive static electric charge built-up in the helicopter. It would discharge through the hook, seeking any ground available, including me. So, wearing a pair of wool mitts plus two pairs of leather overmitts, I'd try to slap the cargo net's steel cable eye firmly into the lowered safety hook before the jolt knocked me and the eye away. When I succeeded, Joe would gun the motor and try to lift the bundle. Sometimes it was too heavy and he'd have to release the hook and I'd unload some of the junk from the net. Other times he would slowly lift it off and fly away with the load swinging wildly, the helicopter swaying all over the sky like a drunken overfed seagull.

Watching the Hughes 500 disappear to deliver its cargo to Parkin, I considered my survival chances. I became a little alarmed realizing that should the helicopter crash, it could be a couple of weeks before anyone would come looking for it. And when they did, they might find the chopper, but who'd know to even look for me? And where? I didn't know myself where I was – except I was somewhere on the Eagle Plains, surrounded by muskeg, blackflies and tiny black spruce, with only a sandwich and a pocket knife. And no place to hide from bears. I definitely should have brought a much bigger knife.

Understandably I was very happy to see them return forty minutes later. We'd only done a few hours of work when clouds began moving in. So we returned to the cabin to have a hot lunch and assess the situation. It started to snow, so we hung tight. *Lunch* dragged on and eventually became *tea time*, then *supper*. At twilight, we looked out on three inches of fluffy new snow and a snowy owl perched on the helicopter rotors. Time to open the bar and hear some real war stories.

The big white wait

By next morning there was three more inches and a hundred-foot ceiling.

"So much for finding the garbage," I said.

"Let's go home," said pilot Joe, but of course we couldn't go anywhere with the clouds so low.

"Can you radio anyone for a weather report?" I asked him.

"Nope, the radio's broken."

"What?!"

"I didn't have time to get it replaced before I came from the Wells," he said glumly. "You guys didn't really want me to show up a day late, did you?"

"How about flying over the clouds?"

"No artificial horizon gauge. Can't descend through the clouds. We would be in a white-out," he said. "*Damn*, I sure wish we could leave this hole!"

At least he was being paid a guaranteed four hours a day at $300 an hour whether he flew or not. And Tom was making his cost-plus percentage. I was the only one not guaranteed any wages. If we didn't work, I didn't get paid, except to cook. Not a clever arrangement on my part. I discussed this with Tom before preparing breakfast and insisted on an eight-hour minimum. It was either that or he could go hungry, I said. What the hell, he smiled, this is cost-plus, so you can have ten hours, and how about Kahlúa on our pancakes this morning?

When the clouds lifted to 200 feet late in the afternoon, Tom and Joe took the helicopter off to gather firewood for the heater. With chopper rental and fuel costs, that was sure going to be deluxe wood. Then we settled in for some poker and ate all the canned oysters.

The next day was the same. The clouds were still too low until about an hour before dark. Then it was too late to make the 300-mile trip to Norman Wells in the remaining daylight. Dawson was an option, albeit a risky one, but Tom figured we'd all go to the Wells because that way at least the helicopter would be going to its home base. We two could fly to Inuvik and on to Whitehorse via commercial jetliner. That was fine by me. I was looking forward to seeing more of the Yukon and N.W.T., specially on someone else's dime. I was getting used to shrugging my shoulders and mumbling *cost-plus*.

The night sky was beautiful. One could see millions of stars and traces of the Northern Lights flitting faint red. The owl was gone, likely off hunting mice or hare.

On Friday we were boxed in by clouds again. When a hole opened in the early afternoon, Joe flew us to the edge of the Richardson Mountains, but we had to return when there was no break in the weather front stalled above the mountains.

"Tomorrow we *have* to make it!" Joe said angrily as he shut off the motor.

"How come tomorrow's so special?" I asked.

"Saturday night there's a party in Norman Wells," he shouted and stalked into the cabin. "I really *hate* this place!"

In search of Norman F.

Saturday the clouds were still there but a bit higher when we woke.

"Let's try to go under it," Joe said, though his voice had lost some of its cockiness.

"I'm tired of staying here," Tom agreed. "All the candy's gone."

We loaded up once again and belted up, three across the front, fuel drums and gear on the back seat. Tom sat in the centre with the map on his lap. In the right seat, there was nothing for me to do as we flew except watch them as they pointed at the map and out the windows towards mountains in the distance and some creeks below. Soon we were over hills, then over a meandering river. Tom was tapping the map and there was much head nodding, but we could all see the cloud-topped mountains ahead.

Hundreds of miles away, on the other side of this formidable barrier, was the Mackenzie River and the small town of Norman F. Wells, as Joe called it. The *F* stood for exactly what you figured. The settlement had the same middle name as most of the North's towns. Inuvik was called Inu-f**king-vik by the bush pilots. Their creativity knew no bounds. As we climbed and the mountains and clouds closed in on us, I could only hope this pilot's flying skill was also limitless.

Clouds seemed to lightly touch the white mountains, their wispy edges fingering the wind-packed snow and glacier ice. A stubble parade of scrawny pines marched vainly towards the summits. The blackness of the tree bark was all that gave dimension to our vision, the rest was fathomless, intoxicating white. Onwards we were hurled by our space-egg past the last trees and into the whiteness. White with no meaning, no distance, no shape. White like the darkness. A total white-out.

Seconds passed – I think they were seconds – for if time is distance divided by speed, and we had no distance, no speed in that void, where was time? I could feel doom looming ahead and around us, with its white arms wide to receive us.

Without warning Joe suddenly twitched his controls and turned the copter around tightly, our bodies feeling the change although our eyes could tell nothing. I stopped breathing. Did he know where the peaks were, how close we were? Searching desperately, I finally spotted far-away-below the dotted limit of tiny trees almost lost in cloud. Joe must have seen it at that moment too because he aimed us down towards that flecked line of re-assurance. We followed them back to the foothills, back to the valleys.

"*Sonafabitch*," Joe said finally, speaking loudly to be heard over the cabin noise. "It's sure hard to tell which way is up in that cloud without an artificial horizon gauge."

"How *do* you tell?" I shouted from my far seat.

"Look at the altimeter," he said. "If it is increasing, you're okay, but if it is going down you could be flying upside down… Maybe."

That *maybe* concerned me. How many white-outs *did* they get in Viet Nam, I wondered.

"Let's try the next range," Joe said calmly. "I *really* want to get back."

Tom flapped the map, then ran a finger over the swirls of contour lines and pointed at a mountain. "That could be this one or this one here. There's a creek marked here but there should be a little bump there…"

On they chattered as we wound our way through the mountains, well over an hour following a snakelike path, turning back at clouded passes, broaching others with a thousand feet to spare. Then Tom turned the map around and looked at the mountain beside us. "Doesn't fit," he said dramatically. "Doesn't fit!"

Joe then grabbed the map and spread it on his lap, studying it between arms outstretched to the control sticks. He glanced outside and back to the map, glanced at the compass, loudly muttering, "Compasses aren't worth a damn up here anyways! Too close to the magnetic pole. Way off!" Then he turned the map 90 degrees and, looking out the window, said, "This valley there looks familiar." He pointed to a rock face and said, "I've seen this somewhere before, but I don't know where…."

Right then we spotted an orange metal shed, surrounded by fuel barrels, perched on an implausible cliff ledge like it was in a TV commercial for new cars.

"A forestry cache. Just what we need," Joe announced while softly setting down beside the blue barrels. "There should be JP4 in one of those."

Our gas gauge read less than one-quarter full. With urgency, we ran around in the crisp air, crawling over piles of drums, wiping snow off faded stencils with cold hands, looking for the magic letters JP4. We found none. How anyone could land a fixed-wing plane on this precarious perch was beyond me, but all the fuel was aviation gas and not jet fuel as we needed. This must be a relay cache.

We glumly pumped the contents of our four reserve 10-gallon drums from the backseat into the main tank. That boosted the gauge to read just over half, and put our range at about 180 miles. It *might* be just enough, *if* we could go straight to the Wells. A big *IF*.

"Too bad there is no sign here to tell us our location," Joe said and both Tom and I looked at him aghast. So he was still lost! Joe admitted he'd been unaware of any cache in this region and the site wasn't marked on the topographical maps. But he assured us he knew what general direction to head if only we could find a way through these mountains.

Forty minutes and three false passes later, Tom handed me the map and said, "You try." Tom had lost all his bravado. He looked as frightened as I felt.

I looked at the altimeter, and the peaks around us, but couldn't find a match anywhere on the map. This might not even be the right map sheet. And we didn't know how to get back to Parkin for more fuel.

In desperation, I shouted to Joe, "All these creeks flow eventually into the Mackenzie, don't they? That, or into the Eagle and then the Porcupine River? Let's follow one. Any one! At least we'll be going somewhere out of these mountains!"

He nodded and descended steeply. "Okay. But we may not have enough gas," he replied without a trace of his trademark grin.

At first the creek was just an indentation in the snow. Then it became a tight creek valley that merged with another and another. Ten minutes later our waterway was a rushing river, cascading through a narrow green-walled canyon, splendid beyond description. The sun's low angle was accentuating the rock bluff and gave the copper-green almost a translucent glow.

"I know I've never seen *this* before," Joe called out. "I'd like to come back someday to look this over… With more gas next time," he added, pointing to the gauge. We traded glances.

I passed them each an apple and then settled back into my seat to wonder where and when our next meal would be.

From the few glimpses we got of the sky through the cloud cover, it seemed we were headed almost due north. We had broken out of the mountains and were cruising down over a wide, meandering river that snaked across a vast plain dotted with hundreds of tiny frozen lakes and swamps and hatch-marked with survey cut-lines. No snow here yet, I noted, with relief. The tracks of cat tractors were everywhere on the plateau, destined to last in the disturbed muskeg for centuries. The river's edges alternated between wide gravel strips and eroded clay cut-banks. Still using the altimeter as a guide, I tried to locate us on any river at the 1,000-foot elevation level. Nowhere did the pattern of river bends correspond and I was feeling quite alarmed.

"I just can't find us anywhere, Joe," I said. "We can't be on *any* of these rivers."

"You're better at cooking than map reading," Tom said, then asked Joe about the fuel. "What happens?"

"At two minutes fuel left, a panel light comes on," he stated. "Then there's a horn that honks and a flashing cabin light that means *land immediately*. There's probably a minute's grace."

"What do we do after we land?" I asked. "How about your emergency locator beeper? We do have one of those, don't we?"

"Yep, we can set that off and jam all the radio frequencies for miles.

That should bring one hell of a search… If any planes are in the areas. And if it works."

"Hope it works better than your radio and compass," I said.

"We'll soon see," he said. "The panel light is flickering. Look for a good place to land. And camp. We may be here a while."

We were approaching a wide gravel bar with a stand of big spruce on the bank above it. I began pointing towards it. Then, out of the corner of my eye, I saw a white *Vee* of waves tight against the far bank. I looked at it hard, squinting for resolution and in the fading sunlight decided it was two Vees, one following the other, both pointed up stream. Perhaps a large rock's wake and eddy in the current?

"What's that?" I yelled. "Maybe it's a boat!"

Joe swung the chopper around as the horn came on. *A-oooogah! A-oooogah!* The cabin light started flashing its warning. Now we could see a dark pointed shape, surely a boat slowly chugging up the channel, leading a second one. We hovered over it, Joe flashing our landing lights at the startled lone boater while the rotor blast whipped the water around him. The second boat was being towed empty. Then we swooped off and landed on the bar.

I swung open the plexiglas door and hopped down onto the gravel with Tom right behind me. We ran, hunched over at first until we cleared the whirling blades, to the water's edge and yelled to the boatman who was already veering our way.

As the round-faced, parka-clad native skillfully swung his boats into shore and threw me a rope, Tom called out, "Where are we? Where are we? We're lost!"

The man looked a little bewildered.

"Twenty miles from Arctic Red," he said slowly. "You are twenty miles up the Arctic Red River from the village."

He explained that he was a trapper headed for his trapline seven miles upriver. This was his last trip from the village with supplies before freeze-up; he was the year's last traffic on this river. And, no, he hadn't trapped on this line before, it was the first time in seven years that anyone would be using this area. He agreed to spend the night with us and take Tom to Arctic Red for fuel in the morning.

"Better make a big fire," he said. "I've got no sleeping robes. They're in my cabin."

We thanked him and pulled his boat bows up and tied them to stakes we pounded into the gravel with his axe. Then Tom and I headed for the chopper to unload the food and sleeping gear. Our saviour, who gave his name as David, soon had a stick fire roaring and was felling a tall dead tree.

"Stand back," he said. "This is going to land right by the fire where you are standing."

Tom and I retreated twenty feet and watched as David's tree fell exactly where he'd predicted. He strode along the trunk, swinging his axe smoothly and effortlessly, chopping the tree into long lengths to feed the fire. Then he disappeared into the woods and returned with an armful of spruce boughs. We followed his example and soon had four soft thick mattresses to lay our down bags on. I gave David my blanket and big parka so he, too, could bundle up warm. He laughed and said he'd slept out before in much colder weather with less clothes, but thanked me.

Together he and I made supper, soup first, then fried potatoes and beans and tinned bacon. David didn't cook on the direct fire, but pulled coals towards him with a stick and set the pan on that. "Takes longer," David said to me with a wink while stirring the food, "but doesn't burn."

As we ate fruit cocktail, passing the can and spoon around, Tom un-bagged a mickey of rum and offered it to David, who looked surprised.

"No, thanks," he said. "I don't drink." And then he added after a long pause, "Well, I drink sometimes, but it's not a good thing. I was supposed to make this trip yesterday but I couldn't, I was too sick." He smiled at us, "Hangover, you call it. I guess it is good for you guys I came today instead."

He curled up against a log wrapped in my blanket. Very tactfully he hadn't belaboured the fact we had been 300 miles off course.

The air felt nippy on my nose and cheeks as I lay in my bag near the fire and watched the trapper fall asleep. Above us, the clouds were breaking apart and the stars began peeking through; a glow in the east would be the rising moon. As the fire flickered on the stones and reflected off the now-immobile helicopter, I experienced a relaxing energy. I felt much safer with our native friend than I had with all our fancy expensive machinery and $300 an hour sophistication.

"Good night, David," I said to the sleeping figure across the fire, "and thanks!"

Though he never opened his eyes, I thought I saw a hint of a smile form on his lips.

Rocketman

It took Tom and David most of a cold rainy day to motor downstream to Arctic Red River and then back against the current. They were dog tired and stiff when we helped them from the boat and handed them mugs of hot coffee. Their cargo, two faded-blue 45-gallon drums of JP4, would see us safely to Norman Wells, Joe assured us. He'd made the flight from Arctic Red to the Wells dozens of times. Can't get lost; all we had to do was follow the Mackenzie River.

We pumped fuel into the chopper, leaving the bottom two inches that were mostly rusty water.

"Everything'll be okay now," Joe assured us. "But too bad we missed that party," he added, his grin back.

We loaded David's trapping supplies into the helicopter and flew them to his cabin so his boat ride upstream would be faster. Tom also wrote out a cheque for $100. "For wages and a day's rental of your boat," he said.

David shrugged, pocketing the paper slip without looking at it.

Then we parted: David at his boat's stern, a dark figure standing by the motor, parka hood pulled back, eyes carefully reading the river current and scanning the shore for game, while we three white guys in our shirtsleeves rocketed south-east at 140 miles an hour, perhaps thirty times David's speed.

Hurtling over the evergreens and muskeg, cap on backwards, confirming our position on a different topo map, Joe grinned confidently as he piloted his craft over familiar territory. I looked out my side window, as though watching a travel movie. There were no smells, tastes, sounds or touches to experience the land we were passing – only sight. There was, in abundance, the throbbing power and wizard gadgetry of aerospace technology. We could soar, we could dive, we could gobble fuel and spend a fortune rocketing without passion, passively riding a shockwave of sound and turbulence. We could fly our machines for a lifetime and only meet the land through our follies – and then, what did we learn?

How might I have grown heading out with David to his trapline instead of coming to the Wells? If he had offered, would I have accepted?

Just as it was getting dark, we saw in the distance a sparkling cross-hatch of jewel-coloured shadows of rectangular buildings. Then the air-strip lights at Norman Wells. Moments later Joe buzzed the control tower and landed us beside the hanger.

I quickly hopped down, walked away from the noise and danger and stood still, watching the stars and collecting my thoughts. It certainly felt good to be on firm ground again with no more helicopter flying ahead. The relief swept through me as it had when David had rescued us.

Joe, having shut off the engine, was carrying his pilot's dufflebag toward the parking lot.

"You looked like you were scared out there," he called to me, "but you didn't have to worry. You were flying in the best with the best!" And he flashed his teeth.

Tom was right on his heels. "Grab your pack," he said. "We'll unload the rest tomorrow morning. Tonight we'll stay in the hotel."

"That'll be an experience, I guess," I replied, "and probably expensive."

Tom just winked and said, "Cost-plus! Steaks, drinks! Everything is on the company. Keep the receipts." His contractor swagger was back big time.

So I hustled to follow them. *Cost-plus* indeed.

3

TRAPPING THE MAD TRAPPER

Corporal Arthur B. Thornthwaite (left) was in charge of the Old Crow detachment during the manhunt. Special Constable Johnny Moses participated in the final shoot-out.

Cpl. Thornthwaite with four canine members of the Force. The dogs wore padded collars and were attached in tandem (single file).

TRAPPING THE MAD TRAPPER

Old Crow nurse's 1932 account reveals how Yukoners sealed Albert Johnson's fate

"... When J [Albert Johnson] had camped at Fort McPherson – where he bought the canoe – he gave an exhibition of his shooting ability. He put 3 ft. sticks in the sand on the river bank & with a pistol in each hand he shot the top off of each stick, crossed his hands & shot again & and kept repeating that. The Indians say about 1 inch was shot off each time. I do not know at what distance this was done..."

>   –   Mrs. Helen Thornthwaite,
>   Old Crow, Y.T., written in February, 1932

The Mad Trapper of Rat River must be rolling over in his Arctic grave. There have been an armload of novels and histories, then a Western B movie called *Death Hunt* loosely based on Albert Johnson's dramatic seven-week battle with the RCMP, trappers, Indians and flying ace Wop May. One might have thought that this 80-some year old case would have been exhaustively investigated. But tucked away in the Yukon Archives, there is a little-known, 4,800-word account of the Depression-era chase that provides fresh insights. For the first time, the RCMP's moves to block Johnson from escaping across the Yukon were spelled out in detail, written from first-hand accounts given by participants of the manhunt only days after the final shoot-out.

In 1983, when retired RCMP Sgt. Arthur Blythe Thornthwaite of Victoria sold his collection of photographs and 16mm home movies to the Yukon Archives [Calgary's Glenbow Museum bought his beadwork souvenirs], there were seven foolscap sheets – handwritten both sides – inside the parcel. Thornthwaite had been corporal in charge of the three-member Old Crow, Yukon detachment during the Johnson hunt. The notes were written by his late wife, Helen, to summarize their interviews with five members of the police posse when they returned to the remote Arctic village.

The story, written like a letter home, is full of detail and emotion. The men Helen Thornthwaite questioned were Constable Sid May and Special Constable (Guide and Interpreter) Johnny Moses, plus Peter Moses and his son Stephen – all from Old Crow – and Peter Lexee [Alexie] who was a Peel River Indian.

Peter Lexee claimed to have spoken with Albert Johnson at Fort McPherson when the man first came by raft down the Mackenzie River in the Northwest Territory. Lexee's account, as recorded by Helen Thornthwaite:

> "Three Indians, seeing him, went over to shake hands
> – usual custom – but he was not sociable. He bought a

canoe from some Indian, bought grub & lots of ammunition at the Company Store. He would buy one article
& pay for it with a $20 bill & pocket the change. Then
he'd walk around & look & buy something else, paying
for each thing as he bought it and always with a new $20
bill. He said he intended to go up the Rat River portage
over to the Bell River & settle & trap at the head of the
Porcupine."

But Johnson didn't do that. Instead he built a cabin on the Rat River:

"... he had dug the floor deep so that half of the cabin
was below the surface of the ground & you had to step
down when you went in. Then he dug even lower in one
corner & built his bunk over that. He could stand up in
that hole & look out from under his bed & he built his
bunk of heavy logs clear down to the ground. Then he
cut peep holes, all around the cabin – he was really inside of a double fort."

On New Year's Eve of 1931, Constable Alfred King, investigating
other trappers' complaints against Johnson, was shot in the chest when
he tried to serve a search warrant at Johnson's cabin. The trapper would
soon have need of his fortress.

A patrol from Aklavik led by Inspector A.E. Eames came to avenge
the near-fatal shooting of their comrade, but couldn't flush Johnson from
his cabin. Helen Thornthwaite described the police patrol's situation:

"... [Johnson] had cleared quite a space around his cabin
& the minute a man would step up on the clearing he'd
shoot. He had a regular arsenal ... Outside it was 60 below. Those three men had already come a long distance

& should have been tired and cold. It's quite foggy and misty at that temperature. You can't shoot with a mitten on & the minute bare skin comes in contact with metal it freezes to it – not in a minute but right now. Well, they held on for 72 hours before they gave up."

As a last resort, Eames elected to blow up the cabin with dynamite. The blast blew much of the roof off and the concussion should have knocked Johnson out. Still wary, Constable McDowell:

"... tied a flash light to a long stick & Eames climbed to look in a corner of the roof when McD would hold the light in the doorway (the door was blown off). The Indian was back with the dogs. He thought he heard two shots but the white men only heard one – but the flash light was shot away & Eames up in the corner was shot through the parka at the neckline and some skin went with it."

Eames retreated to Aklavk for reinforcements and more supplies, issued a territory-wide call for volunteers, and sent an alert to police to the west of Johnson in case he fled into the Yukon. The message was radioed from Aklavik south, then telegraphed to divisional headquarters in Dawson City in the Yukon, where it was wired to Anchorage, Alaska for re-broadcast to the isolated northern post at Old Crow. "A telegram was also sent to Fort Yukon – in case we missed the radio message," noted Helen Thornthwaite. "The telegram cost 35 cents. The delivery – by dog team – $175.00."

Corporal Thornthwaite's assistant, Constable Sid May was off on an extended dog team patrol with Special Constable Johnny Moses, leaving Cpl. Thornthwaite as the only white man in the village of Old Crow.

The Thornthwaites figured that, if Johnson did flee westward from the Northwest Territories, he could cross over the mountains and take one of three choices: "head up the Porcupine [i.e. going southward] for Eagle, Alaska; down the Porcupine [west] for Old Crow, Rampart House and Fort Yukon [Alaska]; or over the top of the Rocky Range to Crow Flats, the north coast & on to Siberia. Crow Flats is 90 x 100 miles & real bush country – with only 4 men on it. Our flat strip [is] 30 miles wide & only one white man [Cpl. Thornthwaite], and toward Eagle a large country with two white men 55 yrs and 67. And so we sat."

Corporal Thornthwaite immediately spread the alert:

"A.B. sent word from here to all the people in the district – one team went south to the head of the Porcupine where Rueb, Bill & Mrs. Bill Mason were. There were also two Indian families there. 300 miles [distance of the trip]. They were scattered from 3 to 6 days apart while it took 5 to 7 days to reach the head of the Porcupine people. Another team went north to Crow Flats. Four white trappers & one Indian family there. The 3rd team went east. That's LaPierre House. There were 3 white prospectors and the Indian family of one of them half way between here and LaPierre House while at La P.H. itself there were the 2 Jackson Brothers, white and a few Indians. Also some Indians & their families hunting between here & the 3 prospectors. They were all told about Johnson – that they should not try to interfere with him nor hinder him from taking food etc. but to hitch up quickly as possible & notify the detachment here at Old Crow."

"[Cst. Sid] May came home & after resting himself & the dogs a few days, started out for the usual La Pierre House & Eagle River patrol. We heard nothing & thought the Police at Aklavik had caught J."

Though they certainly tried, the Mounties couldn't catch their man. For four weeks, in brutally cold conditions, Albert Johnson played hide-and-seek with posses of trappers, Indians and Mounties, amazing them with his ingenuity and endurance:

"[Johnson made] snowshoe tracks – he'd circle all around making big loops a mile or two across but never once coming back all the way to the old trail & never crossing it. The men knew what it was but had to follow it for it's all willow country – you can't see over them – they are that high but you couldn't climb & have a look around either."

Finally Johnson ran out of patience on January 30th:

"[Constable Edgar] Millen and this Parson were following the trail when Millen was shot. Both men dropped & P began firing – about 40 shots – there was no answer – pots and pans flying at every shot so he thought he'd killed J. He pulled Millen along & packed him to camp but M was dead. They went back to get J but J wasn't there – this is what happened. J had made his trail & looped [drawing of a spiral in margin] about a mile &

Peter Lexee witnessed Albert Johnson's handgun shooting display when the trapper first arrived in the Northwest Territories.

come back to near the trail & made his camp so he could watch the men pass by. He dug a hole into the snow going down about four ft – spread a few willows in the bottom & an eiderdown robe … then he put a piece of white canvas across the top of the hole & the men said you couldn't see it 10 ft away.

"All of his camps were made that way. After he discarded the eiderdown only willows were used. They never could tell – by examining the campsite – if he had eaten or even made tea. When he shot Millen he went head first into the snow & tunneled through for about 100 yards & sat by a stump watching them."

The Thornthwaites heard a radio message that evening that Constable Millen had been ambushed and killed by the fugitive. They knew the extensive manhunt would be stripping the Mackenzie valley of meat and fish for dog food. Peter Moses and his son with their dog teams were immediately dispatched to LaPierre House. They had with them 400 pounds of extra dog food and instructions for Constable Sid May and his guide Johnny Moses to join in the hunt over in the Northwest Territories. Trapper Frank Jackson, a veteran U.S. Army sharpshooter, went with May and the three Moses men while prospector Harry Anthony came into LaPierre House to direct operations there.

A new alert was circulated by dog team to everyone in the district: Johnson had killed a policeman and was thought to be mentally deranged. Some outlying families moved into Old Crow and LaPierre House settlements where they would be safer. Loaded guns were kept close at hand.

Helen Thornthwaite's account makes it clear the police posses on the N.W.T. side was having a rough time:

> "... It went to 68 or 70 [degrees below Fahrenheit] every night and believe me, folks, that's darn cold without any trimmings, but they had a strong north wind too. [Cst. Sid] May had to shoot two dogs. The snow would rub against the inside of their legs & make them raw – in spite of all the care May could give them, and [Inspector] Eames even fed every dog a piece of tallow at midnight – they froze the raw spots. Eames thought it would be better to kill them..."

Despite his super-human stamina and cunning, the Mad Trapper never really had a chance to escape the net. The Mounties were using commercial radio broadcasts and relays of Indian mushers in both territories to limit their fugitive's options. To further stack the odds, the police brought in a ski-equipped Bellanca airplane piloted by World War I ace Wilfrid 'Wop' May, to ferry dog food and look for tracks from the air.

> "The time the plane [Captain 'Wop' May's Bellanca] tried for four days to land but couldn't because of the fierce wind – the men kept fires burning on the mountain to help the pilot sight the landing place. It's always terribly foggy & hazy when it's so cold – anywhere below 55 and the haze hangs low. They had to carry wood for 2 miles up those hills so Wop May could tell the wind by the smoke."

When Johnson confounded his pursuers in the Northwest Territories in early February by climbing over the Richardson Mountains into the Yukon Territory during an extreme wind storm (temperatures between

45 to 70 below), he couldn't have expected the entire population of the northern Yukon was watching for him. On February 10th, Johnson's snowshoe tracks were spotted by a party of Peel River Indians near LaPierre House. Harry Anthony immediately sent dog teams to alert the police. By 10 p.m. the following evening, Peter Lexee reached the Mounties' Barrier River, N.W.T. base camp with the news. He'd travelled 90 miles across the Richardsons in 16 hours, half of it in the dark, another incredible feat.

Harry Anthony had also sent a dog driver racing to Old Crow to alert Cpl. Thornthwaite. The Indian made a typically five-day trip in just three:

> "The next we heard was when an Indian came in & said,
> 'That man come!' We both asked, 'What man?' 'THAT
> man!' & gave A.B. a letter from H. Anthony.
>
> "Harry Anthony's letter said the trail showed that J
> was tired & weak. The Indians had taken Anthony out &
> they examined the trail by flash light."

Once again, Cpl. Thornthwaite sent dog teams out to alert residents across the North that Johnson had crossed over into their territory.

When Peter Lexee arrived at the Barrier River camp with confirmation Johnson was near LaPierre House, he found the posse was already making preparations for some teams to go over the pass into the Yukon Territory, based on Special Constable Johnny Moses's sleuthing:

> "May & Johnny were put to J's trail the day after they
> arrived in camp and our Johnny piled himself with glory
> by following that trail for a while & then calling J's hand
> by saying 'Look – that man go this way (pointing to the
> head of the creek where it climbed the Mt.), he wait for

big wind then he go over – snow is hard – no trail – no
catch em quick.' Johnny meant that J would cross the
ridge of the Rockies & even in good weather it's hard
for there isn't even a willow & wood must be carried for
a two-day trip & they take an easier place than this was.
Even the Indians wouldn't cross there in a storm – but J
did. Well, Eames talked to Johnny when they got back.
And Eames took Johnny's advice & teams were to start
for La P.H. in the A.M. [the morning after Peter Lexee
arrived]."

Wop May's plane had just brought in a load of dog food but couldn't
take off again because of the high winds. Eames stayed behind in camp
to catch a ride to the Yukon Territory as soon as weather conditions
would allow the Bellanca to leave.

It took the police posse's dog teams two days to cross the divide
and reach LaPierre House. The police regrouped at LaPierre House, and
Eames arrived with more dog food on Wop's Bellanca.

"Eight teams started after J following his trail. We heard
from Stephen that the plane was carrying the food &
tents & bedding for all the men which would mean they
could travel empty and fast – but Stephen meant it was a
big one – big enough to carry all that & 6 men. The cold
weather continued. J. had discarded his bed robe & his
trail zig zagged. According to his camps they thought he
had no food."

"[On February 14th,] as the men came around a bend
in the river they saw J. He saw them & ran for the bank
– if he had made it he could have killed everyone right

there but the man in the lead shot ... & it made J turn back to the river – he dropped, began to dig into the snow. He had a big pack & he got behind that. [Army Staff Sgt. Earl] Hersey was in the lead – then May then Eames, Johnny & the Indian Special [constable] from Aklavik. The two Indians ran for the bank behind J but J didn't seem to notice them – kept his eye on Hersey & May & shot just once – Hersey knelt down to reload or something – to aim May thinks because H could have been empty & they are taught to kneel & shoot. Anyway J shot – and listen to this – made 7 – seven – wounds in Hersey with the one shell...

"No one knows who killed J. After J shot Hersey he must have caught some movement of Johnny's on the bank for just as Johnny put his head over to look, J aimed at him. Johnny fired & 2 others & J never shot."

"Johnny does not think he killed J but he threw his gun away anyway because he shot at a man with it & now maybe he'd kill meat to eat with it and he didn't like to think of eating meat nor having his children eat meat killed by that gun."

Hersey was immediately flown to Aklavik – in under an hour – where he was operated on and made a full recovery.

The RCMP had never before used an airplane to help catch a criminal. Although Wop May's aircraft had proven valuable by freighting supplies and scouting for Johnson's tracks, the men on the ground voiced their concern about how it may have altered the final gun battle:

"Now just as the first shot was fired, the plane came

overhead. If that plane had come a minute sooner [and tipped Johnson that the posse was close behind], J would have taken cover & been able to pick off each man [out on the river with no cover]."

A detail left out of official accounts, but dutifully noted in longhand by Helen Thornthwaite, was the behaviour of the others in attendance on the 17th of February, 1932:

"All of the dogs were fighting while the men were... 6 dogs to a team & eight teams. Why when one team gets going good it is terrible. Those dogs don't fight pretty. Johnny said they had a terrible time getting the harnesses & toboggans untangled."

Special Constable Johnny Moses gave this description of the dead trapper's possessions and clothing:

"There were notches in one of his guns – a sawed off shotgun – 14 nicks... [Johnson] had on 2 suits of rather light weight underwear, 2 rather light weight shirts, 2 pr. overalls with a bib & a pr. of homemade canvas pants, a blanket parka & a canvas one, 2 pr. thin woolen mittens & a regular cap with ear flaps. His dress alone would show he knew cold countries & how to take care of himself. Nothing he had on was very heavy but it was windproof sort of stuff & he wore two in preference to one heavy article."

Johnny Moses also reported that Johnson had two revolvers in his pack, which would be in keeping with Peter Lexee's account of Johnson's shooting exhibition in Fort McPherson. The police records list no revolvers at all, only a stripped down .22 calibre rifle, a sawn-off shotgun (with notches) and a Savage .30-30 rifle.

> "[Stephen Moses had] talked to the Insp., the Indians & seen a few of J's camps. I asked Stephen, 'You think that man crazy?' & Stephen said, 'Yes! Crazy like fox.' ... Peter Moses is a good woodsman but he said he learned lots of things from that man's camp. ... [Stephen] also told us the plane had 'lots of medicine for that man.' We finally decided he meant tear gas or gas bombs & wondered what the cold would do to them. They had no chance to use them."

Mrs. Helen Thornthwaite was a registered nurse, well liked and respected by the native Indians and whites alike for her compassion and care. She was too much a humanitarian to miss the psychological impact all this manhunting and killing was having on the normally peaceful inhabitants of the territory:

> "When Johnny came down to Crow, he told the folks along the Porcupine – they knew nothing of it [the final shoot-out] of course. The prospector's Indian wife & 12 yr old daughter were alone. Jennie [Lord] was stirring food at the stove but she had her gun in her hand. When Johnny told her J was dead she told her daughter Louise to open the door & threw the gun out. 'Ah too much strong gun (ready for instant action). Long time no want see.' Johnny thinks it was the first night's sleep they'd had for a while."

On 14th July 1983, over fifty years after his late wife recorded her Mad

Four Yukoners who helped stop the Mad Trapper. From left, Cpl. A.B. Thornthwaite, traders Harry Anthony and Harry Healy, Cst. Sid May.

Trapper account, Arthur B. Thornthwaite wrote me the following story in a letter, illustrating a quite different aspect of Northern character:

"Helen worked as a nurse at Hudson Stuck Memorial Hospital in Fort Yukon, Alaska until she and I were married on 5th July 1927.

"In 1929 we became worried about Helen; so she went down[river] to Fort Yukon to see Dr. Grafton Burke. His examination found a condition they were not prepared to take on. Dr. Burke, through the United States Signal Corp at Fort Yukon, sent a telegram to the hospital in California where Arlene trained and gained her R.N. [Registered Nurse credentials]. She was flown out to California.

"This part of that story I did not know until much later. Her hospital had refused to do the operation without first receiving the costs in full. They wired the Fort Yukon Hospital with this statement. My friend, Sgt. Curly of the US Signal Corp, took the message to Dr. Burke. Between them it was decided that much time would be lost sending the hospital's decision to me at the Old Crow Detachment, on the Porcupine River, Yukon Territory, so they would consult with Mr. C.D. Hamilton, the manager of the Northern Commercial Company at Fort Yukon. He and his wife were friends of Helen and me. Hamilton immediately said that on behalf of his company he would guarantee the required payment; and would so advise his head office in Seattle. The operation was performed and Helen was able to come home in the summer.

"That is Northern friendship and the ability to make a far reaching decision when required; I still think that Hamilton probably saved Helen's life."

The cost of the operation was about $3,500 – a small fortune in those days – plus the flights were another $1,500. Thornthwaite was able to repay Hamilton's company from money he had recently received from his father's estate; Hamilton had not known if the young corporal and his wife had any money saved at all.

4

LOVE STORY FOR LUCY

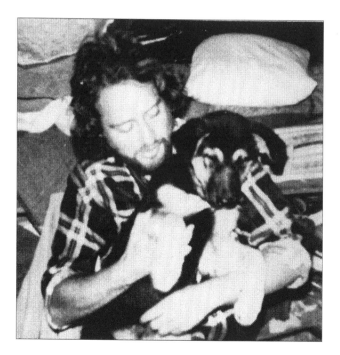

My new companion was a furry-fat black puppy with floppy ears and thick sloppy feet. I hoped she'd grow to be a strong sled dog.

LOVE STORY FOR LUCY

Many, many years ago, my partner Greg Skuce placed a *LOST* advertisement in the *Whitehorse Star* when his puppy Maggie ran away. The next day, an Anglican minister tourist found a young dog wandering around Miles Canyon and promptly delivered her to Greg. She did not come close to matching Maggie's description, but Greg thanked the reverend gentleman for his trouble and said he would take her to the dog pound himself. However, Maggie failed to materialize and little Lucy crawled into his heart, and he began to change his mind.

The first time I saw Lucy – she didn't have that name yet, of course – she was a furry-fat black puppy with floppy ears and thick sloppy feet, sitting beside a puddle of her own pee on Greg's warehouse floor. "What'll we do?" Greg asked me. "Shall we keep her?"

"It looks to me as if she's already decided," I laughed as she started chewing on his pant leg. We partners had acquired a new sidekick.

Somehow she became mostly 'my' dog. Greg went off to Alaska for a week and I was left to house-train Lucy and teach her *come, sit* and *shake-a-paw* and all the other important dog words. She learned very quickly, and I began to wonder if this piglet-shaped bundle was perhaps from German shepherd stock. The colouring matched – she was mostly black with brown eyebrows and paws and there were signs of a shepherd's fierce loyalty. Whatever she was, judging by the size of those feet, she was going to be BIG. We guessed her to be just weaned, perhaps six weeks old, when found. That was mid-July.

In August, Ralph Nordling and I set off for Johnson's Crossing to go moose hunting on the Teslin River. After a dusty, two-hour drive with our friend Jon in his 3/4-ton truck, we were at the launch ramp. Ralph and I each had a small fibreglass canoe, and planned to drift with the current, hoping to add a half-ton of moose meat as we floated to Dawson City. Each of us had our dog along – Lucy with me and Ralph brought his puppy Babe. Babe looked like a spaniel mixed with black lab, with a silky black coat and happy, bouncy disposition.

"Have a good trip!" Jon yelled, waving goodbye as the current caught our boats and swung us round and off downstream. Lucy climbed up on the gunwale for a look around. She walked to the bow and peered long and hard over the port side, her hindquarters high in the air and her head thrust downward, nose sniffing and forehead wrinkled in concentration. After a moment's deep thought, she decided not to venture onwards; instead she retreated, backing right over the other side and into the cold water. Kersploosh!

Up came a sopping furry struggle and then she sank again. Up she bobbed a second time, but only for a quick flurry of splashing. The third time she surfaced, I was able to scoop her with my paddle and flip her into the canoe – a cold, matted huddle of scared and sorry dog. There she would stay a long time, licking her fur and slowly regaining her composure before venturing forth anew. But she had learned something and never fell in again. Back on shore, though, Jon almost fell in he was laughing so hard.

Babe and Lucy were early risers, something neither Ralph nor I could honestly claim. We would sleep late in our nylon tent until the sun was well up and baked us out of our lodgings. The dogs, however, soon learned how to speed up the process: they pulled out all the tent pegs and collapsed it on us. By the time we struggled out of our claustrophobic cocoon, they would be a quarter-mile down the beach chasing butterflies.

For fourteen days, we floated the Teslin and Yukon, and never tired of our furry entertainers' antics.

Back again in Whitehorse, weeks passed and soon September was half-over. Nightly frosts had killed the mosquitoes and the crisp air was just right for hauling in winter cordwood. But when a job opened working out-of-town, I grabbed the chance to earn some quick cash. As there were no vacancies on the survey crew for rod-dog or chain-puppy, Lucy stayed behind with friends in town. Greg had recently taken her for rabies and distemper shots at the RCMP station, and with spring long past, distemper hardly seemed a possibility. I was far more worried about the dog catcher finding her running loose.

"You be good, Lucy! And stick around," I hugged her as I left. "See you later, little buddy!"

She looked at me intently with her big brown eyes, not wagging her tail, somehow knowing she wasn't coming out on the river this time.

The next ten days seemed to whiz by. We were working near Stewart Island just as the geese migration reached its peak. Even over the whine of chainsaws, we could hear the incredible honking of up to 300 Canada geese flying low overhead in a great Vee formation. At times we could count up to 30 of those patterns winging their way south, covering the sky from horizon to horizon.

But while the colours of the leaves were changing around us, dramatic changes were happening faster back in town. Young Lucy had lost her spunk. Her appetite was waning and she began watering at the eyes and nose. A switch in dogfood brands interested her for only one meal and she began to lose weight and strength noticeably. After a few more days, she began to howl at night: erratic, sudden bursts of high-pitched puppy cries that woke friends and neighbours alike. Then she abruptly stopped and drifted back to sleep as if she'd only been scared in a dream.

When I returned there was another problem. My friends were being evicted, partly because of Lucy's noise. I felt terrible because of Lucy's sickness and also because of the problems she had caused. They shared my anguish, feeling somehow responsible for Lucy's condition in my absence. Luckily they were able to find a better place to live immediately, and I returned to my cabin outside town and turned my full attention to my little companion.

I cooked her dogfood in milk and added vitamins, saving her large scraps of meat from my supper. She only ate a bit but offered me a paw to shake. I hoped she was improving. While she slept that night, covered in a blanket in her little doghouse, she was shaking, with a distinct shiver in her jaws. Watching by moonlight, I heard her yelping in her dreams and saw her churning and twisting body – the sounds and motions of fright and confusion. I stroked her neck as she writhed, trying to comfort her until her eyes opened and the panic abated. Those soft dark eyes, shiny under the moon's light, looked tired and afraid. She stared at me vacantly, showing no recognition, then closed her eyes and was asleep almost instantly.

Three more times that night I awoke to hear her delirious yelping, slowly realizing what needed to be done in the morning. In those days, there was no accredited veterinary doctor in the Yukon so I carried Lucy into Whitehorse to a woman who ran a small animal clinic. She agreed that Lucy must have distemper but abhorred the idea of putting her to sleep.

"You don't murder a person who gets pneumonia, do you?" she said and recommended some medicines. "Use these and wait a week," she added.

By evening, Lucy could barely walk. Her balance was so bad that she stumbled into trees and her strength was hardly up to supporting her weary body. Her jaws were shaking more frequently and her mad yelping was no longer confined to night-time. It was tearing me apart to listen. Her suffering was wrenching my heart.

I got my .22 rifle from the cache and looked for ammunition. One solitary bullet was all I found. I looked everywhere but there were no more. One shot was all I would have – it would have to be from point-blank range, face-to-face.

I put the single charged shell into the magazine and went to where Lucy lay shivering beside her doghouse. Her food was untouched and she had fouled herself, but hadn't the strength or will to move away from the stench.

With my one free arm I tried to lift her but she seemed heavy and too awkward to manage gently. She tried to raise herself but couldn't, her wild wet eyes huge in delirium.

"It will be okay, little Lucy," I whispered softly, "not long now."

Twenty yards I walked down the path, laid down the rifle and turned to bring Lucy. Then I saw her.

She was staggering, falling and then pulling herself up and forward again, struggling down the path to follow me. She was so pathetic, yet so valiant, this loving faithful shepherd puppy, her matted fur crusted with pine needles and excreta, her eyes and nose gleaming wet in the sun. My eyes went cloudy with tears and I felt my mouth and face distort with emotion. I knelt to hug Lucy and stroke her tired face as the tears rolled down my own.

How could I shoot this dog I loved so much? I couldn't, and carried her into the cabin to lie beside the stove on a blanket. More pills I fed her, pushing each one into her throat and holding her mouth shut with one hand while massaging her neck until she swallowed. I made beef broth soup and she managed to drink a little. She soiled the rug but I didn't scold her, knowing her pain. Perhaps she is past the worst, I prayed, but didn't believe my hopes.

That night I hardly slept at all, and when I did there were dreams of Lucy painfully struggling, stumbling and falling down the path to follow her master. I'd awaken covered in sweat. For many hours I lay there, listening to Lucy's laboured breathing, always expecting the insane yelping to begin again, wondering how much longer we could both go on. I was scared and felt my insides knotting with each whimper she made.

At dawn, she was a miserable sight. Her jaws were clenching and unclenching spasmodically and her eyes looked sunken and sore. She couldn't lift her head to drink. Those dark brown eyes seemed to have known only horror: they weren't the same soft Lucy eyes that had danced and sparkled on the Teslin River or had laughed and played learning to shake-a-paw. I think Lucy as I knew her was already gone.

Quietly I picked up her limp body and cradled it in my arms. At the door I tucked the .22 under my arm, and walked quickly down the path. Fifty feet away I laid down my bundle softly under a tree. Slowly I worked the rifle's action, then slid the safety off and placed the barrel's end behind her ear.

"With only one bullet," I reminded myself and forced myself to not look away as I squeezed the trigger. Then I dropped the rifle and turned away, closing my eyes until the only thing I could see was the memory of Lucy walking towards me, and I cried like I'd lost my only friend in the world. I cried and felt so very lonely.

ACKNOWLEDGEMENTS & NOTES

My thanks to Jan 'JanBro' Brault and all my other companions (people and the dogs) for keeping me alive and energized out in the Yukon bush. Thanks to friends over the decades who have reviewed my writing and offered advice and encouragement – including my late aunt Marg Gerrard, my siblings John, Jill and Nora, my late parents Eric and Pat, Klaus 'Pancake Man' Ollmann, Dave Jack, Marsha Batchelor and so many others. Thanks also to the late Sgt. Arthur Thornthwaite for granting me access to his photos and Helen's story, and to the Yukon Archives for preserving that collection.

The stories in this book were written in the 1970s and revised in late 2013. Although most writers now use the terms *Native* or *First Nations person*, I have retained *Indian* because that was what Danny and Abby Roberts called themselves at the time.

BRUCE T. BATCHELOR

Bruce Batchelor lived in Canada's Yukon during the 1970s and early 1980s, travelling extensively throughout the territory, fascinated by the wilderness and the people who chose to live in the bush. His Northern stories have appeared in magazines and newspapers, and in the books *Yukon Channel Charts, The Lost Whole Moose Catalogue* and *Nine Dog Winter*. He is also author of *Book Marketing DeMystified*.

Bruce is an editor and publisher, living in Victoria, BC, with his wife Marsha, their son Dan and a gentle black dog named Browser.

Made in the USA
Charleston, SC
05 February 2014